PRAISE FOR
A Mystical Practical Guide to Magic

"This is one of the most straightforward (and that's coming from me), organized and direct books on magic that I've read. ... Aliza is honest, funny, and asks the questions that folks often forget after years of magical or tarot practice. This book is a delight, just like the author."

—Melissa Cynova, author of *Kitchen Table Magic*

"Aliza Einhorn's delightful *A Mystical Practical Guide to Magic* is akin to cozying up in your favorite café with your favorite witch friend, the one who knows all the good stuff and always has your back. Besides presenting an easily accessible overview of the metaphysical arts, this wise and welcoming book offers a veritable cornucopia of magical tools to help you take charge of your life. It's the perfect guide for new seekers and budding witches everywhere!"

—Kris Waldherr, bestselling creator of *The Goddess Tarot* and author of *The Book of Goddesses*

"Magic. It's something we hear about, but what is it? Aliza Einhorn knows the answer to that question. In *A Mystical Practical Guide To Magic: Instruction for Seekers, Witches & Other Spiritual Misfits*, she pulls back the velvet curtain to reveal everything you need to know for crafting a magical life. Aliza is like the cool witch next door who spills the mystical tea while serving you a cuppa. This book offers a lot without being overwhelming. If you're curious about all things spiritual and witchy, this is the guidebook you'll want to grab first."

—Theresa Reed, The Tarot Lady, author of
Tarot: No Questions Asked—Mastering the Art of Intuitive Reading

"Aliza Einhorn is the real deal! In this world where mentorship and guidance is often distant, cold, and electronic, Aliza invites you to take a personal journey, talking to you like a mentor should, as one who has been there living a real magical life and doing so with humor and creativity as she guides you through a mystical landscape. If you are looking for one book to answer all of your metaphysical questions, you have the wrong book. If you are looking for one book to inspire all the right questions and catalyze your own journey to answer them, then you've struck gold."

—Christopher Penczak, author of *The Inner Temple of Witchcraft*,
City Magick, and *Buddha, Christ, Merlin*

"This is an impressively wide-ranging mystical guide by Jewish witch, Aliza Einhorn. Penned in highly engaging prose, her book is an eminently practical guide to those wishing to engage with the spirits and magic in ways that relate to everyday concerns. As an expert on Santa Muerte, I especially appreciate the way in which she approaches the Mexican folk saint of death with humility, respect, and awe. Aliza's book belongs on the top shelf of all seekers and spiritual misfits."

—Professor R. Andrew Chesnut,
author of *Devoted to Death:*
Santa Muerte, the Skeleton Saint

"In *A Mystical, Practical Guide to Magic,* Aliza Einhorn supplies the tools and provides a roadmap that enables readers to achieve their fullest magical and spiritual potential. She shows us how to integrate all our occult interests from tarot to astrology to witchcraft and more into cohesive and profound personal magical systems. Reading this book feels like spending time with a fun and trusted friend. You will wish to return to it over and over again. Highly recommended!"

—Judika Illes, author of *Encyclopedia of 5000 Spells*
and other books devoted to the magical arts

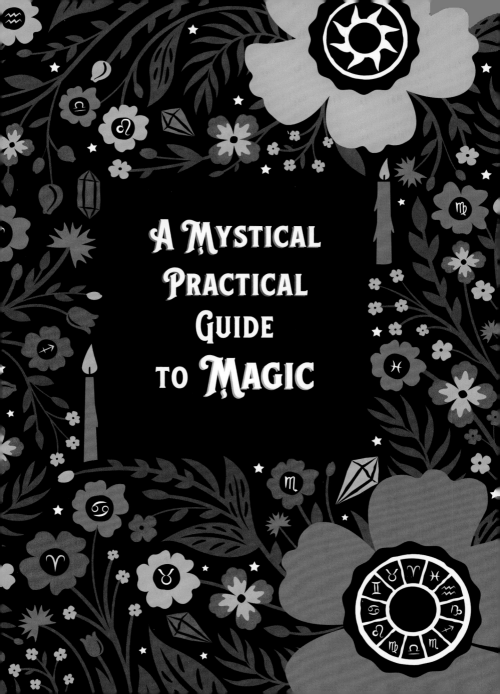

A Mystical Practical Guide to Magic

© Dana Goldstein

ABOUT THE AUTHOR

Aliza Einhorn fell in love with astrology twenty years ago and it changed her life. Her tarot obsession led her to magic, and she uses all three in her work with clients and students around the world. Aliza is a poet and playwright, with an MFA from the Iowa Writers' Workshop. She is planning a return to her literary roots while Saturn is in Aquarius. Find her on Twitter @moonplutonyc, Instagram @alizaofbrooklyn, and at her site, moonplutoastrology.com.

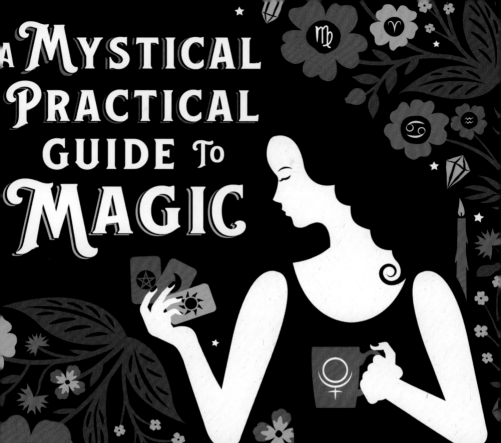

A MYSTICAL PRACTICAL GUIDE TO MAGIC

INSTRUCTIONS FOR SEEKERS, WITCHES & OTHER SPIRITUAL MISFITS

ALIZA EINHORN

LLEWELLYN PUBLICATIONS • WOODBURY, MINNESOTA

First Edition
First Printing, 2021

Book design by Donna Burch-Brown
Cover design by Shira Atakpu
Cover illustration and interior illustrations by Yulia Vysotskaya / Deborah Wolfe Ltd.

Llewellyn Publications is a registered trademark of Llewellyn Worldwide Ltd.

Library of Congress Cataloging-in-Publication Data (Pending)
ISBN: 978-0-7387-6507-5

Llewellyn Worldwide Ltd. does not participate in, endorse, or have any authority or responsibility concerning private business transactions between our authors and the public.

All mail addressed to the author is forwarded but the publisher cannot, unless specifically instructed by the author, give out an address or phone number.

Any internet references contained in this work are current at publication time, but the publisher cannot guarantee that a specific location will continue to be maintained. Please refer to the publisher's website for links to authors' websites and other sources.

Llewellyn Publications
A Division of Llewellyn Worldwide Ltd.
2143 Wooddale Drive
Woodbury, MN 55125-2989
www.llewellyn.com

Printed in China

OTHER BOOKS BY THIS AUTHOR

The Little Book of Saturn (Weiser)

For Dana, Elana,
Avigayil, and Lyone,
and to all my beloved
students and clients.
This one's for you.

And to Jewish
Witches everywhere.

CONTENTS

The Invisible World

Real—Life Magic

Ritual

Moon Pluto Magic

HOMEWORK: LITTLE EXERCISES, BIG SUGGESTIONS

ɐNTRODUCTION

Most of us have at least some notion of what the word *spiritual* or the phrase *spiritual path* means, but have you ever stopped to define it for yourself? To make it more clear. To know what the hell it means to you.

Your definition of *spiritual* doesn't have to include words like *enlightenment* or *consciousness*. Mine usually doesn't. A spiritual path isn't necessarily the big fat truth of life for all beings everywhere for all time. It's more personal than that. It's the big or little truth for *you*, for your own magnificent, meaningful life.

We're all doing it: seeking, searching, wandering, wondering, flying, driving through our own personal heartland, whether you use those words or not. If you're alive, if you're reading this book, you're heading somewhere, even if that somewhere feels like around and around in circles. This book is here to help you through it. It's a practical and sometimes personal guide to some of the things that helped me craft my own spiritual life over the decades, and how to work with those things in daily life. I didn't set out to create anything though. It happened naturally, intuitively. My feelings led the way.

WHAT DOES A SPIRITUAL PATH INCLUDE?
FRIES OPTIONAL

A spiritual path, no matter how informal, will likely have tools and strategies, signs and clues, mysteries, rituals, beliefs, sometimes rules, things we do once, things we do over and over, all to help us understand better who we are, where we are, why we are, who we're meant to be, our life purpose, and even what happens after we die, if anything. And then there's the day-to-day business of living. That's spiritual too.

All the clues, tools, and strategies in this book can help you explore all of the above, bring you new questions, and make you think. They are tools to help us probe the mystery of our lives: where we're going and how to get there, alternate routes included. We may not get all the answers in the time frame we desire (right now!), but I've got travel instructions for you, stories and rituals for the road. I'll be using this metaphor every so often: the road, the map, landmarks, detours, everything we need for the journey. We start in Tarot Town but then we keep on going. And since I'd just moved back to New York City as I started writing this book, the city, too, will guide us, its subways and streets, cafes and seasons. We are never not somewhere along the way. The streets speak.

Also, a spiritual path of any kind, like this book, is here to comfort you in your distress or crisis, your dark night of the soul. The way I see it, your spiritual path or journey, your exodus, your metaphysical restlessness is the poetry of your life: noticing the details all around you while asking the big questions.

YOUR COLLECTION OF COOL STUFF

Right before I started writing, I hit on a phrase to summarize what the spiritual path is for me: a collection of cool stuff. It's my way to describe the strange and not so strange things I was drawn to over the years, the things that stuck around. I chose them or they chose me. I'm pretty sure you have a collection of cool stuff, too, your influences and inspirations. Maybe you don't think of them that way. Maybe it's just "who you are," but I bet those things and ideas that you fell in love with made you feel connected to something larger than your own small shadow in this big world. Perhaps their presence grew dim at times, but you didn't forget, and they were company through the long hours, like good friends. Everything in this book is a friend.

Your collection of cool stuff might be in a shoebox under your bed, on a bookshelf, or in your head in the form of a to-do list. Maybe your collection has been buried so long you don't even know what's in there anymore because your family or friends or partner or culture wouldn't understand. None of the things I mention here (astrology, tarot, talking to the dead, to name just three) belong to any particular faith or religion or tradition. They belong to us all.

My hope is that this book will inspire you to dig into your own personal collection, excavate it, no matter how ancient it is, no matter how seemingly forgotten, and that you head out on your own spiritual road trip to the great wide open and beyond, like the Fool card in the tarot who is always starting over.

A Jewish Witch

In 2014 I started announcing on my blog *Moon Pluto Astrology* that I was a Witch. I was already an astrologer and tarot reader and doing both for a living. This was a few years before witches got trendy and showed up on social media, not just in the metaphysical section of the bookstore.

Witch is an old and complicated word, but it was new and perfect to me. I felt it described what I'd already been doing for years: writing spells, doing magic, healing others, entering trance states, flying on a broomstick (no, not really). And I wasn't just any Witch but a Jewish Witch (the tradition of my upbringing and ancestry of this lifetime). It wasn't strange for me to combine them. I felt like I was remembering what I'd known all along. Jewish Witch? Of course! Hebrew incantations? You bet! Why am I telling you this story? What you call yourself or how you identify is also part of your collection of cool stuff. You get to choose.

Little Maps

Any of the following things and ideas can be part of your spiritual path and/or help you figure out that path. At the end of each section you'll find recommended resources, mostly books, but sometimes not.

Tarot

Tarot is the art of prediction and will also help you grasp past, present, and future, and talk to you about who you are and where you need to be. One difference between astrology and tarot is that tarot is a physical deck of seventy-eight cards with pictures on them. Tarot is tactile; you hold it in your hands, although both astrology and tarot are psychic tools. We read the cards as we read the charts, seeking information, guidance, truth.

Astrology

Astrology is the art of understanding and is, without question, the best metaphysical means for understanding yourself, other people, and your life's purpose. Astrology can help you make sense of the past, survive the present, and predict the future. Sounds good, right? Your birth chart, or natal chart as it's often called, cast for the moment you were born, is a map of you, a mirror. Even a little astro learning goes a long way.

Magic

Magic is the art of doing. There are so many kinds of magic and magical traditions, but here's one thing I know for sure: magic is an antidote to feeling powerless. Another thing I know: magic requires action. Third thing: magic is real. Examples of real magic: A money spell when money is needed. A love spell when love is needed. And if you don't need love or money? There's plenty of other magic out there.

The Invisible World

The Invisible World is the art of seeing, but not necessarily with the eyes. Even before my parents died, I always felt connected to the invisible. By invisible I mean anything, anyone, that doesn't have a physical body the way we do. This could include dead relatives, maybe ancestors, maybe angels, ghosts, pets who left us too soon. I like the popular phrase *spirit guide* as a general term to describe the invisibles. This invisible world, like magic, is as real as you and I.

Ritual

Ritual is the art of routine, which is the art of daily life. It may seem like a dull idea on the surface, but a spiritual path goes hand in hand with a plan. What items, if any, do you need for your spell? How often should you meditate this week? Will you draw a tarot card each day or every other day? All of this is structure and these structures create continuity in our lives. Routines are like leashes around our souls. Feel free to roam but come back.

Writing

Writing is the art of expression. When you write, you find out how you feel, what you think, what you can't forget, where your mind goes. Writing is a way to keep track, keep a record, go back in time. It's like meditation but across a page. With writing, you can beautify your experience and make sense of it too. I used to say that I didn't know how I felt about anything until I wrote it down.

Moon Pluto Magic

Moon Pluto Magic is the art of self-acceptance and is my own home-made magical system for the ones who feel "too much" and get labeled "too sensitive." They need intense creative outlets that match their emotionally intensity. This magic is for the artists, empaths, intuitives, introverts, and anyone who relates to it. Moon Pluto Magic is about you loving you, including the parts that others, or even your-self, have deemed ugly, unnecessary, or worthless. It's healing magic.

THE MAGIC CAFE

I was in a coffee shop today, working on the paragraph you're read-ing right now and thinking how to sum up this introduction and prepare you for what we're going to be talking about. I had more than one coffee shop to choose from this morning, and I take such decisions, and coffee, seriously. After all, it would be an hour or two of my day, a day that could change everything. You never know when magic is on the menu.

That was the name of the place I was at, by the way, the Magic Cafe, and I sat down to tell you this: everything I bring you here is an offering—to help you create your own spiritual, magical, life. Maybe tarot and astrology and coffee shops and Witches are for you and maybe they're not—but it's your destiny to discover who you are spiritually and what you believe, and to create your life and tell the whole wide world about it, if you choose. Maybe you will write your own book and teach us a thing or two about how best to live each day, spiritually, magically, from the heart, your heart.

Much love,

Aliza

September/Elul 2019

TAROT

Tarot is magic.

Welcome to Tarot Town

There's this Hollywood image that I love: the kerchiefed fortune-teller, sitting before her crystal ball at a carnival or beachfront boardwalk. She's got a mysterious, faraway accent and rings on every finger. Her voice is ancient. On her table appear to be tarot cards, which she caresses as she tells you news of your life, your future!

My life as a tarot reader is a bit less cinematic. I work from home usually, doing my tarot readings in the kitchen, in everyday clothes, my cat vying for napping space on the table. Drawing cards (some say *pulling*, some say *throwing*) is normal around here, part of daily life, and yet no less magical.

Double Espresso, Please

I'm at my favorite coffee shop, the Magic Cafe, thinking about how best to introduce you to something I love so much, the tarot, without being too esoteric and without dumbing it down, and the truth is I think it's best if we just jump in.

My mantra: I don't know how the tarot works exactly; I just know that it does. In other words, I'm not a scientist who can quantify why a reasonably intuitive person, like you or me, can know what will happen or when, and yet I've done this for others and had it done for me, time and time again. It's always remarkable but not entirely unusual.

 ## HERE IS AN EXCERPT FROM A CONVERSATION I AM CURRENTLY HAVING WITH MYSELF ABOUT HOW TO ACQUAINT YOU WITH THE TAROT

What is the work or purpose of the tarot?

To answer the questions we ask. To answer the questions we don't.

What kinds of questions do we, should we, ask?

Whatever we want.

If you want tarot to be part of your spiritual path, your quest, your adventure, your collection of cool stuff; if you want to engage with the tarot to figure out whether it *should* join your life, know this:

Tarot is a tool for divination (predicting the future/fortune-telling) but can also bring you insight about your life. It all depends on what you ask and how you ask your questions. Tarot is a window, an entrance, a gateway, something we can look through to get the information and answers we seek.

"But I don't have any questions," said no one, ever.

You Create Your Own Storm

During one of the first tarot classes I ever taught, a student asked about sleeping with the deck under her pillow so that the luminous mysteries of the tarot would find their way into her head while she slept. I liked that she assumed, or knew, that there was something special about this pretty deck of cards.

Now what I'm about to tell you is a theme that will travel through each section of this book: what brings you epiphanies and powers and intuition and gifts blossoming is *practice*. Might that practice include sleeping with the deck under your pillow? You can give it a try. But lightning tends to strike in a storm, and with any spiritual quest or path, you create your own storm. In other words, you have to do the *work*.

I'm not saying that the cards won't whisper to you their secrets, and such stories do become legend, as they should, but what I'm telling you here is mystical *and* practical. If you want to know tarot, you have to get to know tarot and *let tarot get to know you*. Make it part of your everyday life.

Detour: A Very (Very) Short History of the Cards

In that same tarot class, we talked about the supposedly enigmatic origins of the deck, including one theory that it was brought to earth by aliens (I hope it's true!), but also what appear to be the facts: its appearance in Italy in the mid-1400s and as an actual card game developed for Italian royalty. Some tarot scholars pinpoint the 1700s (these are big swaths of time, I know) for when tarot transitioned from mere game to oracle, cartomancy. But no matter the creation story

(and details vary depending on whose book you're reading), tarot cards over the generations became a device for telling fortunes and eventually that beachfront-boardwalk lady was throwing cards to let you know if and when a tall, dark stranger was on his way to you with an offer of true love.

THE LEAST YOU NEED TO KNOW

First and foremost, the tarot is a deck of cards. It is a *thing*, an object. And you do things to it, like touch, shuffle, cut, arrange, lay out, throw across the room when annoyed. You can hold the deck in your hands, spill coffee on it, get it dirty, keep it clean. You can enfold tarot decks in your clothes as you pack your suitcase for the Arctic. It's a thing.

Second, tarot is a process, a system for seeking and finding information about *anything*. Should I meet a friend tonight? What do the cards say? What is my life purpose? What do the cards say? I mean it when I say you can ask the cards anything.

Some don't *ask* of the tarot. They demand. I have done such in times of great drama or stress. Tarot, tell me what I need to know or else! Do the cards laugh at our obsessions? Sometimes. But don't be afraid to pour your passion out. The two of you, you and the deck, are in a *relationship*.

Third, tarot is a pictorial system. These cards aren't blank. They have images on them and numbers too. The images and numbers have meanings. They even have suits like playing cards (tarot's precursor). Focusing on these pictures, along with your question(s), allows your conscious mind to relax so you can find the answers you seek. It's that gateway or entrance I mentioned earlier. The cards help you get out of your way. The cards help you *see*.

Also, through working with the tarot, you may, with practice, refine your intuition to the point that you won't even need cards, but I'm getting ahead of myself here.

THERE ARE AS MANY TAROT QUESTIONS AS STARS IN THE SKY

Reading tarot cards for self-reflection or insight is not the same as the "yes or no" type of question. Instead, we are looking to explore a situation or ourselves, profoundly, as fully as we can. Every tarot reading is a journey. We want to get somewhere. We want to feel satisfied, satiated. Where a yes or no question can feel like a peck on the cheek, a question seeking insight is a long, slow kiss.

That said, I find the best and most fun tarot readings have elements of both. It really depends on what you want at any given time. I've also seen wily folks try to "trick" the cards. They have a yes/no question in mind (will I get the job?) but ask it in a roundabout way in an attempt to outsmart the cards. They think being indirect will win them a better answer. Honey, I've seen it all.

A typical yes/no question: is that cute person whom I gave my phone number going to text me? A question seeking insight: am I ready for love?

The first one appears quick and easy. The second one clearly is not. Which do you prefer?

Why Choose Tarot for Your Spiritual Path?

Of course, I'm biased, but tarot is so good at what it's supposed to do, so good at bringing clarity *and* confusion, I think everyone should try to work with the cards, at least for a little while. See if you like it.

- Do you like interesting pictures with layers of symbolism?
- Do you want to bolster your intuition?
- Do you want a portable question/answer system that is sometimes maddening?
- Do you want a fortune-telling oracle with a curious history? Tarot is for you.

You can return to the tarot over and over, although it's not a religion. There are conventions or customs, sure, but not laws. It can help you figure out who you are, where you are, what you want, how to get there, what to do—there's lots of "what to do" type questions in my own damn life—all through this question/answer process.

THE SECRET TO READING TAROT CARDS REVEALED.

How to Read Tarot Cards (in 900 Words or Less)

So, you want to read tarot cards, and you want to read them fast and easy. These days nobody's got time to waste. I can tell you how to do it in 900 words or less. In fact, I can tell you in one word. You ready? That one word is *practice*. (You may remember we met this word in the previous chapter.)

What is *practice*? Something you do over and over. Something you do with persistence and consistence. That's it.

But is that *all* there is to reading tarot cards? Of course not, but it's one of the most important tarot lessons of all.

Every Picture Tells a Story

It's not even fall yet, and I have a window open. The first open window of the season. It's still August in the city, in Brooklyn, and this morning, after a six-mile walk from my neighborhood to the next, I get a call from my sister, happy about tarot. She just bought her first deck and is excitedly telling me how you don't have to memorize *anything* to read the cards. You don't have to buy a single book of simple or complex card interpretations (i.e., what the cards, supposedly, mean). You can just look at the pictures. Pictures tell a story.

I tell her about an artist friend I used to have, a fellow tarot lover, who is a far more visual reader than I'll ever be. She sees fine detail, sees color, sees line. I tell my sister, still glowing in her newfound tarot love, that there are infinite ways to read the cards. Pulling apart the picture is one way. Just make a habit of it. Every day, if you can.

LITTLE BLACK BIRDS LIKE SWORDS IN THE SKY

In the tarot there are four suits, like a regular deck of playing cards, but here we have Wands, Cups, Swords, and Pentacles. Each suit is associated with an element and most of my decks are arranged this way: Wands/fire, Cups/water, Swords/air, and Pentacles/earth. A couple years ago, I was putting together a tarot class and noticed these little black birds showing up from card to card in the Swords suit in the famous Rider-Waite-Smith deck. Have you seen it? This deck has inspired tarot lovers all over the world for decades, and when I talk about a particular tarot card in this book, I'm referring to this deck. If I hadn't been teaching that class and gazing at each card, though, I never would have noticed those pretty birds.

I tend to see the bare minimum of any image. My intuition quickly takes over. Is it possible that the eyes absorb more than we realize? Maybe, but the journey from eyes to brain to intuition is lightning fast. It's like I know what the card means, what the card is saying, even before I see it. Or mere seconds later. But we'll talk more about intuition in the next chapter of this section.

ꟻOR THE ℒOVE OF ℛACHEL ꟼOLLACK

It's totally legit to be bookish about the cards too, to decide that you want to read them and interpret them the way your favorite tarot author does. There's no shame in learning from the greats, like Rachel Pollack and Mary K. Greer, to name two. There's no shame in memorizing their card meanings, what they say in their books, and never straying. Maybe you like the idea of a lineage. Real-life tarot schools exist, but tarot isn't a monolith and it's not like we get initiated into tarot. I mean, our favorite authors and experts are the closest we've got to gurus, if a guru is what you seek.

With all the tarot books I have (and that number is many, but not too many to count), I admit that I mostly skip everything in a book (exercises, history, the author's philosophy of tarot) and head straight to the card-meanings section, if there is one. Once in a while I remember what I read. Most of the time though? I forget until I pick up a book again.

ꟻAST, ℰASY, AND ℕEAT

These categories aren't always so neat but some of us *do* have a primary method of reading the cards: visually like my artist friend, or book-oriented, or more by gut feeling, with the cards commencing intuitive hops. We may read different ways at different times or use a combination of techniques, but we're always taking the cards and running with them, somewhere, into the field of the unknown, where the answers are. After all, that's what the tarot is for, to help us find answers.

Which method is best for you? To answer this question, please return to the first point of this chapter: practice. Practice and find out. You won't know how to work with the cards, how *you* work with the cards, how you *want* to work with the cards, until you do.

Can one learn how to read the cards quickly? Some folks want to know the secrets of the universe in an hour. Others don't mind thirty years. Learning tarot falls somewhere in between. Regarding easy: it's easy if you enjoy it. If tarot gives you pleasure, as it did me, it's the easiest thing in the world.

I Have a Question for You

I'm back at the Magic Cafe as I write to you. It's still August, the air still sweet with the promise of leafy fall weather, and I'm thinking about where to take you next. Uptown? Downtown? Here are two questions: *Are you psychic? Do you want to be?*

NEXT STOP

FIND A FRIEND.

TAROT WILL
MAKE YOU PSYCHIC

The next thing to do in Tarot Town is make a friend, a tarot friend.

How it works: You ask the cards a question. They ask the cards a question. You pull cards for them. They pull cards for you. Simple.

I was almost going to qualify it. I was almost going to say: You can hit the tarot jackpot on your own, without ever reading cards for others. But the truth is you can't. Not in the way I'm talking about here.

••• HOMEWORK •••

FINDING A TAROT FRIEND

You want to make sure your tarot friend is intelligent, trustworthy, and open-minded. Intelligent because you are too and tarot isn't just mystical fun (not that mystical isn't intelligent). Trustworthy because you may be sharing some secrets (and they will be too). Open-minded because not everybody is into this stuff. You don't want somebody making a sour face while you whip out your cards at the cafe. And, of course, they need to be tarot-curious, or already a tarot lover. They don't have to be wildly, passionately obsessed with tarot, but definitely choose someone who won't mind if that happens.

Then what you do is:

1. take your tarot friend
2. to a cozy place (public or private)
3. and read the cards (and read this entire section for thoughts on how to do this).

Tarot Jackpot

Knowing things you have no way to know. Psychic ability. Wildly expanding your intuitive powers. Tarot was made for this! And to get close to mastering this skill, you need this tarot friend, an honest one. Someone to say: yes, you were right, or no, you were wrong.

Dear reader, there will be very few things in this book where you'll hear me say YOU MUST or YOU HAVE TO in all caps, but regarding this point, I'm firm. Even if psychic ability isn't your main focus with the cards, most folks want to know a little something about their future and the future of their loved ones (and their enemies, but that's another story). It's a human thing.

In fact, I don't think I've ever had a student who didn't want to develop and increase their intuition. It may be a more universal desire than even the desire for love. I've known plenty of folks who live like happy hermits, alone in their stone cottages, but nearly everyone asks me this: *What's next?* That, my friends, is a psychic, intuitive, predictive, fortune-telling question!

Also, there is a limit to how objective we can be about our own lives. There is a limit to our hope, to the potential *good* we can see for ourselves, especially if we are asking the tarot emotional or meaningful questions, when we have something at stake, which is pretty much every tarot question, even the seemingly silly ones. The questions matter or we wouldn't be asking.

1–800–Are–We–Going–To–Get–Back–Together?

I use the words *psychic* and *intuitive* interchangeably a lot of the time, although the word *psychic* for sure has some negative connotations. We think of charlatans and 1-800 phone lines where fake (or even genuine) psychics charge you an arm and a leg by the minute.

Bottom line: psychic or intuitive ability is not rational. It's not logical. It can't be explained. It's not even the same as being a student of human behavior. What you're doing is seeing the future (or past or present) no matter what word we use. This is not the same as seeing your kitchen table—although it kind of is, just with a different set of eyes.

Here's an example. Your tarot friend asks this question: Are my girlfriend and I getting back together? You pull a couple of tarot cards and you do your thing, whatever that thing is, however you read the cards, your own particular style, and you tell your friend the answer.

"Yes," you say. "You will get back together." Cue mysterious music.

You hear back from your friend a week later. They were in touch, went on a date, and moved in together! You were right, accurate, spot-on!

This practice of question and answer, of asking the cards, of getting verification, of exercising this muscle is what makes the muscle stronger. Does it make it perfect? No. Are road trips perfect? No. Sometimes we run out of gas or get a flat tire. Accidents happen. Sometimes we take too long at the truck-stop diner and get delayed. But we get back on the road and we keep going.

SWAMP TAROT

When I was living in Florida, I did exactly what I'm suggesting you do here. I got myself a tarot friend. This town was nicknamed the Swamp because of its sticky, humid weather and wildlife—snakes, alligators, possums. The town was as wild as the tarot itself.

We started a club of two, the Swamp Tarot Club, and we met once, sometimes twice a week at our favorite restaurant, usually sitting at the bar, to pull cards for each other. *Will this happen? Will that happen?* It was easy to judge our rightness or wrongness because many of the questions were about the near future. Sometimes we asked bigger, more metaphysical questions or questions with more

distant time lines. Week after week her intu-
ition grew. I'm sure mine did too.

My friend was a newbie, so she got herself a deck (we mostly shared mine at the
bar), and she even read the little book that
came with it, but the primary way she
learned to read tarot was week after week
making predictions for me and for herself
and also comparing the cards. Did we get similar answers for the
same questions? It was a process that unfolded over time.

By the way, I do not recommend reading under the influence,
although once we were done, it was red wine for me, basil martini
for the lady. Our weekly ritual.

A More Detailed Example
from the Swamp Tarot Club

QUESTION: Will I get the job?

Friend takes cards. Shuffles them. Friend cuts cards, placing
them in five piles from left to right. She then neatly puts the cards
back into one pile, starting with the stack nearest her and randomly
putting the other stacks below it.

She takes the top card then and flips it over. Damn. It's that
sorrowful, dramatic Three of Swords, which shows three swords
plunging into a heart. You see the card. She sees the card. You may
not get the job.

Now, your reader may feel and say, "Absolutely not. It's a *no*."

Or, she may hesitate and feel and say, "Well, there is some kind
of issue here, some sadness. It's not a straight line from desiring and

applying to getting it. Something gets in the way. And it hurts. I'm so sorry."

YOUR PSYCHIC ABILITY IS LIKE THE SUBWAY

Go with me on this, even if you've never taken the New York City subway or any subway.

Obviously, a train takes you from place to place, subway stop to subway stop, and your job is to be a good passenger and exit the train when you reach your destination. Sometimes the train skips stops though (at least in New York it does).

Your intuition also has potential stops, like the subway. For example, you may be doing a tarot reading for someone, or for yourself, and you intuit an hour into the future or a month into the future, or even a year. This happens to me when I read cards. Someone may be asking a question about *right now*, but I get visions of *seven years* from right now.

Perhaps we are leaving Brooklyn at the Borough Hall station and we get out at Wall Street. That's close, near future. Union Square, however, is farther away and is the more distant future in the metaphor here, maybe a month, not so far. From Borough Hall to the Bronx though? Even farther. That could be a year away, or more.

My point is the more you work and play with tarot, the more you'll understand how *your* particular intuition does what it does. It's different for everyone. You may not *ever* be able to accurately predict if I got the job I applied for yesterday, but you may see with perfect precision my life ten years from now. Your personal intuitive subway train may skip many, *many* stops, homing in on a future we can't even imagine—until we see it, so to speak, with our own eyes.

Tarot in the Wild, Tarot in Everyday Life

I'm an urban hiker, always taking long walks in the big city, and I carry a tarot deck with me in my backpack, always. It's seen as many miles as I have. I haven't pulled any cards on the subway yet, but that might be next.

There I was, one fine morning at the Magic Cafe once again. I was trying to figure out what to do about the super and the mail. *Super* is slang for *superintendent*, the caretaker of a building or property.

I had just moved back to Brooklyn and the super used to live in my apartment. He keeps the building running smoothly and safely, fixes what breaks, and has keys to everything because he may need to get into anything at a moment's notice.

What I didn't want him getting into, however, was my mailbox, and he was still checking *my* box for *his* mail. Every day. It didn't make sense. I live here now. And mail, my friends, is sacred.

I mentioned it once. I mentioned it twice. Solutions were discussed but nothing changed.

My quandary was that I didn't want to alienate the guy whom I might need for any number of reasons, including unclogging a toilet, setting a rodent trap, or even help with carrying a big package up the stairs. But, I also didn't want him going through my stuff to find his stuff. *Here was a job for the tarot.*

See, living with the tarot means that you consult the deck not only during your dark night of the soul, but for everyday problems too. *What to do? What not to do?* Sometimes the questions are one and the same.

If you follow any tarot social media, you may believe that you need to bedeck your tabletops with crystals and plan elaborate rituals and call yourself a Witch to talk to the cards and have them talk to you. But it's not necessarily so. You can come as you are.

You, Too, Can Be a Coffee–Shop Tarot Lady

I hadn't done much tarot reading on the fly in public, if any, since I moved back to New York, but the moment felt right. It was time to whip out the cards. Tarot need not be complicated or heavy. It can be a beam of clarity and cut through your confusion. And although elaborate, multi-card tarot spreads exist

(a spread is a predetermined arrangement of the cards), I decided to pull just one as I worked through my dilemma with the super. One-card draws are great for novices *and* experts.

What card came to say hello? The Three of Wands (from the Rider-Waite-Smith deck, my favorite).

In the tarot, the Wands are one of four suits. It's the dynamic, enthusiastic suit compared to the emotional Cups or the anxious Swords or the practical Pentacles.

The Three of Wands shows a person with their back to us, looking out at a body of water, ships in the distance, one wand to the left and two to the right. It's a bright, bold sunny day in Three of Wands world. The figure firmly, confidently holds on to one of those wands as if to say, *I have arrived. I am here. This is my land.* It implies waiting, patience, but also strength.

The Three of Wands figure isn't focusing on a detail or a literal small thing (like a mailbox in my case), but looking out at a vast blue sea. The big picture.

Look straight ahead, the card said to me. *Don't get distracted. There's something bigger at stake here. And like these ships in the water, this, too, shall pass.*

The drama of the super and the mail didn't get resolved that coffee shop day, but the Three of Wands showed the way. Perspective.

••• 𝕳OMEWORK •••

TAROT FOR YOUR EVERYDAY LIFE

You don't need to be a coffee-shop tarot lady to bring tarot to your daily life. Here are four suggestions.

Keep a Tarot Journal

Keep track of the questions you ask. Keep track of the answers you get. Keep track of your mood and the date and the time. Keep track of cards you see over and over. Keep track of cards you haven't seen in a long time. Keep track if you use a tarot spread from a book or you made one up. Get an ornate journal or something simple. Keep multiple journals. Buy beautiful pens. Journal in crayon or magic marker. Use a totally impractical giant sketch pad that takes up nearly the entire kitchen table (I think I may do this one ASAP).

The Every-Day (or Every-Week) Option

Draw a card in the morning. Draw a card in the evening. Draw a card in the middle of the night and the middle of the day. Think about your cards while you're at work. Let them perplex you. What do they mean? Figure them out. Consult your books. Do a short tarot spread every Sunday. Do a complex tarot spread every Friday. Take pictures of the cards and look at them throughout the day.

Take notes (or not) on your thoughts. Let your thoughts percolate. Draw no conclusions. Close your eyes and hear your intuition.

Tarot with Others

Post your tarot thoughts on social media. You can use a fake name or your real name. Keep track online of your daily and weekly cards. Ask folks to comment. Engage in tarot conversations. A card a day and what it means. A spread a week and what it means. Offer to interpret cards for others. Share your tarot philosophies and how the cards make you feel. Start a tarot podcast (this technology is easier than ever). Make a date with your tarot friend (see "Tarot Will Make You Psychic"). Start a tarot group online or in person. You'll learn the cards and improve intuition no matter your specific intention for the group.

Make Tarot Art

Draw your favorite tarot cards from your favorite deck. Make your own versions. It doesn't have to be sophisticated. Share your creations if you want. Create your own deck with homemade flash cards. Print out tarot images and make a collage. I did this years ago with the Eight of Swords because Eight of Swords was how I was feeling. This card shows someone stuck and all tied up, literally, surrounded by swords in a marsh. I still have the picture on my phone to this day, a collection of Eight of Swords scotch-taped to the wall.

Dear reader, you don't have to pray or meditate or go to a special room to touch and talk to your cards. Or maybe you do. It's up to you. You can bring your tarot to the wild or keep her at home, for your eyes only. Getting creative with her, in a daily way, will bring you closer. What do you think? Is tarot in your collection of cool stuff yet?

I'LL MEET YOU AT THE CORNER OF
MYTH AND TRUTH.
LET'S EXPLORE SOME TAROT LORE.

Breaking Tarot Rules

There's no one way to do tarot. There's no *best* way to do tarot. In this chapter, I want to share with you some tarot lore and tarot questions that have come up over the years in my life as a tarot reader. Even if you are new to the cards, these "rules" may be familiar to you. Much of what I say here is an invitation—not just to break rules but to create your own, do things your own way, an idea at the heart of this book. Please know this is not a comprehensive list of the questions that have crossed my path, but some of the most popular among tarot lovers.

Do I Have to Use Tarot Spreads?

Among the many tarot books that exist in the universe are books of tarot spreads. Even books on other tarot topics often include one or two famous ones (the ten-card Celtic Cross for example). I'm not disputing that tarot spreads are useful and fun, but they aren't required. You can also make up your own—spontaneously or in advance.

··· ꝪOMEWORK ···

PAST, PRESENT, FUTURE: TAROT SPREAD

Here's an example of something simple, but not really. Shuffle and cut your cards. (Or not. It's up to you). Put three cards on the table horizontally. The card on the left will represent the past. The card in the middle is the present. The card on the right shows the future. This three-card spread moves us through time (past, present, future)—which is a wild idea in and of itself when you stop to think about it—and you can apply this spread to any situation when you want to know what was, what is, and what will be. Tarot spreads, even short, simple ones like this, add a little structure to your query. They contain it. They make our questions, and thus our lives, feel more manageable.

Know that you have options. You can be that organized tarot lover who uses a structure every time. You can be the one who makes it up as she goes along, wild and free and random. Got a question? Throw a card! Throw two! Throw ten! And dig into those cards without any predetermined pattern. As I wrote above, you can create your own spreads with their own shape, purpose, number of cards, everything. You can choose.

Should Ꙇ Ꝇet Others Ꞣouch Ꟃy Cards?

First, no one should touch your stuff without asking, but if you start doing readings for people, for friends or professionally, take note of how you feel. Some tarot readers let others shuffle and cut their cards or pull cards from the deck. Some feel the cards are an extension of their body and prefer a hands-off approach.

The bulk of the readings I've done for others have been over the phone, with a small percentage in person, at a bookstore or party, or with a one-on-one client. No matter where the reading took place, I still had to figure out what was best for me, which is: Don't. Touch. The. Cards. Unless I invite you. But that's me. You may feel otherwise.

Along these lines, I had a card reader once hold up his tarot deck to my throat chakra (the middle of my throat), but his cards didn't actually touch me. Not physically anyway.

WHAT ARE REVERSED CARDS AND DO I HAVE TO READ THEM?

No, you do not. Reversals are when some of your cards, or many of your cards, show up in a tarot reading upside down rather than right side up.

I've known famous tarot readers, well-respected, esteemed tarot readers who *never* read upside-down (inverted, reversed) tarot cards. And I've known readers (elite and novice) who do. There is no rule that says you have to. Many books do give interpretations for both.

I've also seen folks advise newbies not to work with reversals, but you may feel called to do it. When I was learning tarot, reversed cards made me feel dizzy and disoriented. I tried reading them for a few months, but eventually I stopped. Ironically, reversed-card meanings are usually my favorite part in any tarot book.

The man who introduced me to tarot *only* read upright cards. He would say that the reversed card had nothing to tell us, and he'd move on to the next. Alternatively, some folks will just turn reversed cards right side up and read them the usual way.

Where Should I Keep My Cards?

I knew a girl (you read about her in "Welcome to Tarot Town") who told me she slept with her tarot cards under her pillow so that the cards would whisper their mysteries while she slept. She asked my opinion about this and I told her that for me the tarot isn't holy. The cards didn't have such powers. They certainly help us during waking hours, yes, but weren't magic in and of themselves. Looking back now, nearly ten years later, I might not be so quick to dismiss her approach or bring her down to earth. After all, I might have been wrong. And sometimes how we feel about things changes. And maybe the cards *are* holy.

Now, I still don't sleep with a deck under my pillow, but where and how we keep our cards matters.

I have one tarot deck, at least, in every room, and I always carry one with me, but usually casually, in a small plastic bag or wrapped up somehow to keep the cards from straying, but nothing fancy. I'm a practical person.

You may have read that you need to wrap your decks in silk scarves and pearls or keep them in a golden box, but again this is a matter of how you feel, what you're drawn to, and your lifestyle. Right now, in my office I've got about ten decks in two spare drawers, mingling together. I do believe it's best to have multiple tarot decks because sometimes you need to switch things up. The cards, like anything, can get stale.

Is Tarot Bad, Wrong, or Evil?

Well, obviously I don't believe so because I'm writing this book, which contains chapters filled with tarot love, and I'm assuming you don't believe tarot is bad either, despite the presence of a Devil card and a Death card, among other intense images. But think of it this way: if tarot isn't holy, then for sure it can't be evil. It's a thing. It's neutral. It's art. Activate it, learn it, use it, and it becomes a tool for divination, self-reflection, everything we've been talking about here. The cards are what we *do* to them. The cards are what we put in them. The cards tell stories. Anyone could take the tarot and use it for nefarious purposes. Most of us, however, are just looking for a little insight into our lives, a little yes and a little no, a little will he text me back.

Can I Buy My Own Tarot Deck?

Yes, yes you can, although I've heard from multiple people over the years that we should receive our first deck as a gift. Even the other day, my sister, whom you met in "How To Read Tarot Cards (in 900 Words Or Less)," was telling me such a story. She has a friend who wanted a tarot deck for years and was waiting for one to fall from the sky (which wouldn't surprise me; stranger things happen). Still, you don't need to wait to buy your first deck or your second deck or any of your 1,000 decks. It won't poison your luck or ruin your readings. You can buy all the decks, as many as you want. Gifts are great though. I'd never refuse the gift of tarot, but it wouldn't stop me from getting my own.

It's the fall equinox now as I write this, late September, unseasonably warm in the big city. I'm wondering what you're thinking as we near the Tarot Town city limits. Have you decided yet? Is tarot for you? If you aren't sure, hang on. There's one more landmark we need to see.

NEXT STOP

A MEETING WITH THE HANGED MAN.

Two Tarot Spreads for Your Travels

It's still September as I write to you, humid and raining as I walk to the subway. The journey of errands awaits. I've got my usual tarot deck in my backpack, an ancient, dog-eared Rider-Waite-Smith. When I post pictures of it on my social media, someone inevitably comments that it looks well-loved, broken in, if not downright needing a bath. Tarot is both personal and communal now. What once was private, between diviner and seeker, or diviner and herself, can now be shared with the world.

Before we say farewell to Tarot Town and head on to our next destination, I want you to meet the Hanged Man, plus two tarot spreads that can help you decide whether tarot should be in your collection of cool stuff.

The Power of a Single Card

You can study tarot for years, for decades. You can study *a single* tarot card for years, for decades. Any of the seventy-eight cards would be suitable. Even after twenty years, a deeper meaning of a particular card may arise for you. The cards grow as we grow.

I started keeping a journal shortly before I moved back to New York. I was worried about the move. Would everything go okay? One evening, I was reading through notes that I took during recent tarot readings—not ones I'd given but ones I'd received. My reader kept seeing the Hanged Man when she read my cards. There was a message, but what was it?

Now, the Hanged Man is known to be one of the most mysterious, curious cards in the deck. Every version I've seen looks about the same. The background colors or Hanged Man's clothing may vary, but not the central image: an upside-down figure hanging by one leg from a tree branch, with the other leg crossed behind it.

What the heck is this guy doing upside down? How did he get there? What does he see from that vantage point? If you decide to study the tarot, you'll learn that what are called the Major Arcana cards (the ones that have names as well as numbers, like the High Priestess or Empress) are rich with symbols, layered, each card like a book in and of itself. This really is what we mean by "reading" the cards. The cards can also be brought down to earth, though, summed up in a gesture or a word.

Of course I'd been acquainted with various meanings for this card over the years, and I'm a pretty good note taker too. I had written down exactly what my tarot person said to me about these Hanged Man moments I was having. It was one word that she gave me, though, a word I'd never come across in my tarot travels thus far for this card. *Faith*, she said. The Hanged Man is telling you *have faith*.

But don't take my word for it. The Hanged Man may mean something else when you see him, and you have to work with the cards to find out.

This isn't the first time we've encountered a one-card tarot story in these pages, but I want to emphasize this point: sometimes one word, like one card, is enough.

••• ℌOMEWORK •••

IS TAROT RIGHT FOR ME? TAROT SPREAD

Here is a two-card tarot spread for exploring whether tarot should be in your collection of cool stuff. Two queries: *Show me what tarot will bring to my life. What lessons does tarot have to teach me?*

Shuffle and cut your cards or just shuffle or just cut or pull the two cards from anywhere in your deck. Discover which method you prefer.

Once you pull your cards, lay them on a flat surface like a table or a desk, but please know that you can draw cards anytime, anywhere, even when you're on an urban hike. The tarot is portable.

One afternoon I was walking through a Florida farmer's market, on the phone with a friend who was hiring someone for a job. I had my cards with me of course, and I shuffled as well as I could while walking. The card I drew turned out to be 100 percent accurate even while strolling in the hot Florida sun.

I recommend you do this spread in the morning and then return to it in the evening. Think about those cards you pulled when you can during your day. Look up meanings in different books for different perspectives.

••• 𝕳OMEWORK •••

ONE CARD, MANY ANSWERS: TAROT SPREAD

Here is an alternate tarot spread featuring my favorite method, the single card. In this one, I want you to ask the tarot *directly* for an answer, rather than using the third person.

First, you want to touch and shuffle your cards a little. Kiss the deck if you like. Hold it against your favorite chakra. If you're unfamiliar with the chakras, hold the deck to your heart or your throat or your belly. Notice what you feel, if anything. Then pull a card from the deck. You can do this sitting or standing or lying down or while walking.

The question for the cards: *Tarot, tell me what you want me to know about working with you, getting close to you, having you in my life, as part of my spiritual path!*

If you aren't sure how to interpret the card, please return to "How To Read Tarot Cards (in 900 Words Or Less)" for some ideas. Keep track of these tarot spreads and their answers in your tarot journal.

𝕳ERE 𝕴S 𝖂HERE 𝕴 𝕮AUTION 𝖄OU, 𝕯EAR 𝕽EADER

If you commit to tarot, you'll start to *think* in tarot. You'll find yourself telling a friend that you've having a Five of Pentacles day (not so great) or a Nine of Cups moment (much better). Or like my sister just said to me, that her life feels like the Tower in slow motion. You'll start seeing tarot people everywhere: Oh, that guy looks like the Two of Pentacles! Oh, that lady has an Empress vibe. The deck will come to life. The images and symbols and meanings will dance around your head in dreams, like the letters of the Hebrew alphabet do for me.

Of course, you will need to familiarize yourself, at least a little, with the deck to get to this point of thinking and dreaming in tarot, but with love and attention comes the tarot looking back at you, asking to be seen.

BACK ON THE SUBWAY

I step off the train and wait for another one across the platform. I notice a man sitting on the stairs, whistling. These stairs lead passengers up and out of the underground subway station onto the streets of New York City. He seems to not be part of this world and I wonder which tarot card he is. The King of Cups, but who knows. Perhaps the Hermit or the Hanged Man. What would your friends say about you? Which card are you?

NOW WE MUST TAKE OUR LEAVE OF
TAROT TOWN AND HEAD TO THE NEXT
STOP ON OUR SPIRITUAL TRAVELS.
I'LL MEET YOU THERE.

RECOMMENDATIONS:
IN MY TAROT SUITCASE

Learn Tarot by **Joan Bunning:** I hope Ms. Bunning never takes down her website www.learntarot.com, which is based on her book *Learning the Tarot: A Tarot Book for Beginners*. The card explanations are written in phrases, not full sentences, which I appreciate. Look up any card online (plus search term "learn tarot") and you'll get a list of her smart, tasty, concise meanings.

The New Tarot Handbook by **Rachel Pollack** is like a trial-size version of her meatier volumes. Her card meanings are *not* identical to Bunning and I love to cross-reference. I also like **Mary K. Greer's** *Tarot for Your Self,* again for individual card interpretations. I particularly love some of her occult-like definitions for reversals. For example, she calls the reversed Queen of Pentacles "kitchen magic"!

The Marseilles Tarot Revealed by **Yoav Ben-Dov:** Although Ben-Dov doesn't work with the Rider-Waite-Smith deck, my favorite, I keep this book close to me always. I love his ideas on how to read the cards, plus his poetic writing style.

Anthropologist Angeles Arrien's *The Tarot Handbook* is another one that isn't Rider based (she uses infamous Aleister Crowley's Thoth deck) but I also love her deep ideas and poetic expression. Even one page (one paragraph!) of Arrien is a full meal, whereas Bunning is the perfect single bite.

Tarot decks: I think I must have at least six Rider-Waite-Smith decks, maybe more. They differ in terms of coloring, card back, card stock, card size. I also have Rider-Waite-Smith "clones." These follow the Rider template but have an additional theme that overlays, like cats or witches. I love to see how an artist remains loyal to the original imagery and also where they reinvent. The more decks you have, the more you can explore this.

The Connolly Tarot Deck is one of my longtime favorites, which is Rider inspired but departs from some of the usual depictions. I particularly love the Connolly Ten of Swords. In the Rider, we see a figure facedown with ten swords poking bloody holes in his (or her) back. It's always a shock to see. In the Connolly, however, a woman is calmly facing us with the swords surrounding her, but they don't touch.

Why so many decks? I'm in search of perfection, for the deck that always feels good in my hands and answers the questions as asked, no fuss, no muss, no moods, no sass (well, maybe a little sass). It's like the dream of the perfect partner. Can such a dream become real? I'll let you know when I find out.

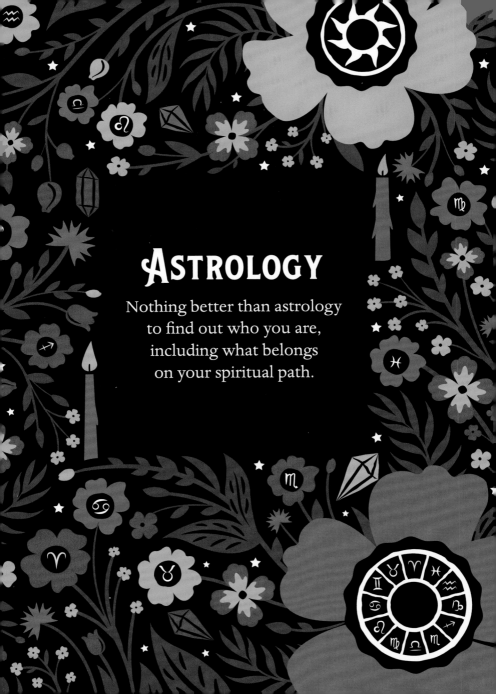

ASTROLOGY

Nothing better than astrology
to find out who you are,
including what belongs
on your spiritual path.

Instructions for the Star Road

Did you ever look up at the sky and feel your heart pound with wonder? You were thinking about those mysteries up there, stargazing. Maybe the Milky Way was keeping a secret for you, or you discovered that bright star one night was the planet Venus in all her resplendent finery. You felt a kind of longing, but it was more than longing. It was certainty. It was truth. The heavens above not only had a message, but more, if you got real quiet and listened long enough in your solitude.

I'm no astronomer. You probably aren't either. We are mystics here and searchers, and in this section I want to tell you the mystical truth of astrology, what it's good for, and why you'll fall in love with it if you give it a chance. I have guidance for how to bring it to your daily life, keep it like a steadfast flame burning. I've worked with the stars for years now, and they came with me on so many journeys and dark nights of the soul, helping me understand myself and others. Don't underestimate the value of understanding, especially during a soul-dark night.

ORDINARY MONSTERS

A New York story: I fell in love with astrology one snowy afternoon, the moment my teacher looked at my birth chart (and we'll talk more about birth charts in the next chapter), isolated this one thing (two planets actually), and explained to me *who I was* in about five words. Impressive, right? This *thing* had been a source of pain and shame to me, my essence basically, and he told it very simply. I wasn't a monster after all (my words, not his), and if I were a monster, I was an ordinary one, just another human who had this, that, and the other in their birth chart.

Astrology is so good at this, so good at showing you who you are, with compassion. Astrology, and a good astrologer, can help you make the most of your complicated, terrifying, beautiful existence. Knowing who you are is essential for crafting your spiritual path because if you don't know who you are, at least a little, how else will you do this holy task?

HERE IS THE WAY I UNDERSTAND AND LIVE ASTROLOGY

The planets have an effect on everything under the stars, from the collective everybody to the most personal, intimate detail of you and your life, from your dreams and your fears to your love, your work, your sex, your death, and everything in between.

Astrology is the sky itself, the planets in their constellations roaming around. The planets *talk* to us. How do they do this? I'll give you more detail later on in this section, but for right now, know this: there's something called a *transit*, and when I do an astrology reading, this is mostly what I'm talking about with people—how the planets now (or in the past or the future) are helping us or, god(s) forbid, hurting.

And, yes, planets like Mercury or Venus, and the signs, like Virgo or Taurus, for example, have particular characteristics, qualities, personalities, needs. You probably already know this. You probably already know your Sun sign and possibly your own birth chart. You know that the Sun in Cancer has a different set of concerns, different consciousness, different way of being than the Sun in Aquarius or any of the other signs.

The sky, however, is little but a beautiful backdrop, a lonely landscape without *our* lives to influence and push against. That's *this* astrologer's perspective, that we need each other.

BACK TO THE SWAMP

Remember my Swamp Tarot Friend from the previous section (in the chapter called "Tarot Will Make You Psychic")? She learned a little astrology, too, enough to gasp when I told her about her current Pluto transit. As with tarot, a little astrology goes a long way, and like a good Sun (and Venus) in Leo, she learned enough of the zodiac to know *her* sign is the best of them all (ha!).

When I left Florida, she was on the verge of a new Uranus transit, which would surely bring her a surprise or two, Uranus being associated with the unexpected. As usual, though, there's a reason why I'm telling you this tale: if you are reading this book, then you have a birth chart (natal chart) based on the day, date, year, location, and time of your birth. It's you, a map of you. This is why learning the foundations of astrology (ideally from a good book and a good teacher) are so important—because that's where most of us start, with our own chart and trying to understand ourselves. To do this, you've got to grasp the core: what the planets mean and what the signs mean, at the very least.

ASTROLOGY IS MAGIC

There are other kinds of astrology too, less personal kinds, like the astrology of current events, looking at the global scene. I know astrologers who read on politicians only or the stock market, but I wanted to get better at life, *my* life. I figured the more I understood *me*, the happier I would be or the more money I could make or the more stable I would feel (wouldn't that be nice).

The best thing about this personal kind of astrology, though, is the birth chart's talent for revealing who we are while answering other big questions: Why are we here? What is our purpose? How do we get there? The planets and signs and their myriad interactions in our birth chart will show it! Is this not magic? (And, yes, each astrologer may have their own sweet or sour take on what they see in your chart.)

If you decide astrology belongs in your collection of cool stuff, you can study as many asteroids and snazzy predictive techniques and eclipse cycles as you wish. You can go above and beyond the foundations that I talk about here in this book and find a speciality so intimate that only you and two other people in the world are the experts! No matter what, though, astrology is here to help us, like the Hermit's lantern from the tarot. It's here to light our way, to show us who we are, how to be better, to find what we're meant to do, and reach our dreams.

YOUR ASTROLOGY WORK

The crux of this section is all about *your* astrology work, how to put an astrology *practice* in your life so you can decide whether you want to make a home for it and let astrology take up space in your spirit, blood, and bones. I'll share what's essential to take with you on the road, where to go first, what to learn next, what to save for later, ideas for good astro-habits so you feel and stay connected. I'm bringing you instructions for the star road because you can work with astrology daily, just like tarot.

ONE MORE THING BEFORE WE LEAVE THIS CHAPTER

I remember like it was yesterday. I heard a story about an ancient astrologer who, while drawing a birth chart by hand, heard the chart *speak*. Really. There it went again. Barely above a whisper. She put her ear close to the table. The chart was telling her where to put the glyphs for the planets and the signs. *Not here. Over there!* Bossy chart. It was as if the chart were alive, not just a picture of the soul, but the soul itself. Stranger things have happened, dear star lovers.

LET'S TAKE A CLOSER LOOK
AT THE NATAL CHART,
WHICH IS A MAP OF YOU.

Your Birth Chart Is a Map of You (Part One)

The previous chapter ended on a mysterious note. I was telling you the story of an ancient astrologer who, as she was drawing an astrological chart by hand, heard the chart speak. Who are we to doubt such tales? Many of the old ways are lost to us.

Dear star lovers, I'm not here to convince you one way or the other, but let's say it was a metaphor, or our astrologer was wide awake through a long night and had a drop too much to drink and was hallucinating wild scenes, including an astrology chart come to life. Even if this version of events were entirely false, there is still an individual person, a soul, behind that chart—with a voice of its own and stories to tell. Why wouldn't it speak?

The Internet Making our Lives Easier

Here is the technical truth. There is free software that will create a birth chart for you, which is a picture, usually in the shape of a wheel, of where the planets were in the sky when you were born. All these placements have meaning, and how they interact with each other also has meaning. Put it all together and we get *you*.

Some astrologers do buy pricey, fancy professional software, but it isn't required. You can visit a website or download a phone app. All you have to do is type in your (or someone else's) birth data: month, date, year, time of birth, location. That's it. You don't even need the time of birth to get a clear picture of a person, contrary to what many believe. (The birth time adds precision, but good astrologers can still get what they came for without it!) Also, many websites and phone apps will even interpret the chart data for you and thus you *never* have to learn how to read or understand an actual astrology chart (or create one by hand).

This is a mixed blessing. It's good because you can start learning astrology right away without a teacher, without books, without a class. It can be less good because then you miss out on the process of doing things by hand, from scratch, the way our forebears did, the ones who could make the chart speak. Also, the quality of interpretation will vary from app to app, and there is a limit to the intelligence of computer software. The human heart, wisdom, and intuition cannot be simulated.

But if you go the software/app route, which many of us will and, I believe, should, especially if you wind up looking up lots of charts, you can still enjoy that sweet process of a chart unfolding piece by piece. How you keep and stoke this magical research chart-building feel is by reading, doing lots and lots of book reading.

Let's say you use a phone app to create a natal chart. That phone app likely has chart interpretations, which may or may not have been written by experts or even good writers, so don't just stop

with those. Ask who are the famous astrologers of each genera-
tion. Read them first. Then read the ones considered to be the best.
Finally, read the forgotten ones, the ones you have to track down
from interlibrary loan. They likely have the most to teach you. With
astrology, there is always more to discover and apply to our lives,
even after departing the novice stage.

FATE STOPPING TO TAKE A PICTURE

Let's bring those metaphors back now. The natal chart is a map of
you, a portrait of the sky, the planets, when you were born. The
planets are always moving, but it's as though they stopped briefly
for the gods to take a picture. Let me explain. You were born at a
particular moment. That sky, that moment, that day, is a reflection
of you, the you that you are and will become. When people see you
that's what they're actually seeing—that sky.

Fate stopped to take a picture and in that picture, we see your
darkness and your light. We see your disappointments and your
dreams. We see your blind spots and deficits and talents beyond
reason. Your birth chart is not only you but has a plan for you. It
shows your life path and gives hints about past and future lifetimes.
It's a book you can read backward and forward, cover to cover, over
and over.

Learning astrology is a course of study, no matter how you do it.
It does require your time and attention. You won't learn everything
in a day, but I know you *can* learn it. A few weeks? A couple months?
Maybe! Depending on your schedule, you could learn many fun-
damental foundational concepts during a season. Pick one. Do you
tend to stay inside more during the winter and need brain food for

cabin fever? Perhaps summer is your time and you'll sit outside in the sun with one of the astrology books I recommend at the end of this section.

In the next chapter, I give a few tips for what to learn first and how, but before we get there, please consider:

1. My suggestions are to get you started. They are first steps, but deep ones. Suggesting that you read such-and-such book because it's a good one and will really help you understand astrology isn't very mystical or romantic, but will give you good bones, a strong start.

2. Understanding the meaning and symbolism of the planets and the signs is where you should begin. It's not that everything else is extra, but without good bones, we can't stand up.

3. Your astrology knowledge is something you will *apply*. For example, you will learn about Aries and the planet it's associated with, Mars, and you'll think about the Aries you know, or maybe you are an Aries. You'll think, *Hmm, is this me? Does this describe my Aries friend?* You'll start to form opinions about the nature of Aries and Mars as you begin to understand how astrology relates to your own life, to real-life, to people you know. I didn't fall in love with astrology because it was some arcane, impossible-to-understand, rarified subject. I fell in love with it because it made so much sense.

4. I learn best from a teacher, in person, one-on-one. It helps me to have information repeated over and over, but in a slightly different way each time. *You* may learn best from a book, a website, a

video, a phone app, an online class, or a real-life teacher. Feel it out. If you're trying to learn astrology and are making no progress, you may need a different method.

PRACTICAL SUGGESTIONS FOR ORGANIZING YOUR ASTROLOGY PRACTICE.

Your Birth Chart Is a Map of You (Part Two)

I've broken down your astrology work into four parts here as though you were using an app or other easy software. I'm keeping it simple so you don't get overwhelmed. Think of this astrology work as your daily (or weekly/monthly) astro practice, something you do regularly.

··· Homework ···

ASTRO TO-DO LIST

1. Start learning your birth chart. Start with words that are familiar to you, such as *Sun*, *Moon*, *Mercury*, and the other planets. You'll see that each planet is in a sign. Sun in Libra. Moon in Gemini. Mercury in Scorpio. What do each of these planets and signs symbolize? What does it all mean? Many phone apps will answer those questions with accessible descriptions and you can also search online, although it might take you a lifetime to read every internet characterization of Sun in Libra or

Moon in Gemini, and much of the information will be repetitious. Find a writer's voice you like and keep reading or stick with an app.

2. Decide when to do this work: each day, each week, or each month. How much time do you actually have? How fast do you want to go? When can you find a little quiet time? Never? Once in a while? Twice a day?

3. Contemplate what other tools to use for your reading and research. Which books to start with? Which websites look good? Make a list of possibilities. I put some favorites at the end of this section.

4. Keep track of what you learn in your astrology journal. You have one, right? You can keep your tarot and astrology findings separate or in the same place. When I was learning astrology, I had many journals going at the same time, cheap spiral-bound ones as well as fancy diaries, to trap every new discovery. I had towers of books and notebooks all over. It wasn't neat or perfect. Does this sound like you?

This is how you'll discover if astrology belongs in your collection of cool stuff—because you will or you won't run to do this work. I recommend a weekly schedule at least, as this will allow you to dig deep into your placements. You are following *a map of you* to parts unknown, disassembling the chart (which is your soul) and then assembling it again, piece by piece.

A Scorpio, by Example

Let's say you enter your birth data into your phone app and it says that you have your Sun in Scorpio in the First House. That week you could just study the Sun in general and what it means in a birth chart. The week after you could read about the sign of Scorpio in a few different reference books. The following week you might discover what the First House means. You could explore all three in one week if you are feeling ambitious, like a Scorpio. And, by all means, search online for the phrase *Sun in Scorpio in the First House*. I do, however, recommend studying each component on its own (Sun, Scorpio, First House) because this way of thinking and research will give you that firm astrology foundation that mere app perusing cannot.

Eventually, you would do this with all the planets and signs (and possibly a few other categories, such as the houses, which I referenced above) and thus learn astrology by first getting to know *yourself*, your individual natal chart.

How are you feeling? Does this feel like something you want to do? Pay attention to any immediate physical reactions.

You could even pull a tarot card each week, asking: Is this a good week for my astrology work? Should I take a break? Should I go even deeper?

••• ℌOMEWORK •••

AND NOW FOR A TAROT SPREAD TO EXPLORE ASTROLOGY'S PLACE IN YOUR LIFE

Pull three tarot cards, one for each of the following three questions:

What will astrology teach me?

How will astrology teach me?

Why should I study astrology?

Answer these tarot questions once a week for a full month in the evening by candlelight. Experiment with reversing the order of the questions, but make sure to pull one card for each. Keep track of your findings in your astrology journal.

For a little extra magic, add up the numbers in your birthday and reduce them to a single digit. If your birthday is January 1, 1911, your number would be 14 and $1 + 4 = 5$. Make sure to do these tarot questions on the fifth day of the month and the fifth day of each week. If you consider Sunday as the start of the week, you would do your tarot on Thursdays, plus an extra session on the fifth of that month.

At the end of the month, make sure to read back the entries in your astrology journal. You can also review as you go. What themes emerge? Did you see many repeating cards? Did you get more or less of one suit? How many Major Arcana? Those cards have names as well as numbers in most tarot decks. Compare the different types of scenes or moods that you're seeing in the cards you pull. There will definitely be patterns. Write down what they are.

NEXT STOP

WHAT JAZZ SINGER DINAH WASHINGTON HAS TO DO WITH ASTROLOGY.

TRANSITS:
WHERE THE PLANETS ARE NOW & HOW THEY AFFECT US

First, a story.

New York City, like life, is a labyrinth. If you want something, anything, you have to follow these twists and turns, a maze of required actions to get what you want—through city streets and subway rides and online searches and morning strolls through noisy neighborhoods, the bodegas opening like flowers in the sun.

On a good day in the big city, you may find yourself with everything going as it should. The train runs on time. The weather is perfect. The coffee isn't too hot and tipping the coffee-cart guy feels like a prayer. You're grateful for the chance to taste that dark drink on your lips. Good or *easy* transits feel like this. Everything going your way. Happy to be alive. You lift your head out of the maze of your thoughts and feelings, and it's the astrology, the sky, the transits (a word I'll define more on the next page) that are supporting you, without making a sound. They're just there, the backdrop to life.

You can probably guess what I'm going to say next, that difficult transits bring the opposite of what I described above: hard times, hard feelings, everything gone wrong. If a transit is hard *and* long (the planets move at different speeds), its influence can take years, transforming us into unrecognizable shapes, pain, howling grief. We may not even know who we are anymore during and after a hard transit. We are forever changed.

Every hard transit has a guardian angel though. There's usually something good going on with *your* astrology while the tough stuff dances on your agony. A saving grace.

LESSONS, LESSONS, LESSONS

Transits are where the planets are now (or in the past or future) and the effect they are having on you *personally*, what they are doing to *you* (or me or anyone). Think of transits as causing the lessons in life. *Lesson* meaning something you have to go through. Fate. Transits show our fate.

For example, Saturn will be in a particular sign for a particular number of years (around three) and doing something particular to you, your life, during that time frame. I remember, a couple years ago, Saturn was giving my personal, natal Moon a hard time. In astrology, the Moon signifies home (among other things), and I had just moved down to Florida and was adjusting to all the changes. Saturn signifies strides made through hard work (also among other things), and I was working (Saturn) on my first book at home (Moon), which was old, cold, and termite infested. It was all very Saturn, i.e., difficult. Also during this Saturn transit, my cat Cleo died (you'll read more about her in "A Tarot Spread for the Dead").

I don't mean to scare you. Not every hard Saturn transit will bring a death, but there's always a reality check. If there's a hole in the roof that needs fixing (or a hole, a "problem," anywhere in your life), Saturn will show you.

Know this: the planets are always up to something in the sky, keeping busy, and always affecting us, whether we realize it or not. Easy transits feel like days (or months or years) of blessing, like much-needed rain in the desert. Hard transits are when things fall apart: health, finances, family, faith, transformations we didn't ask for and most likely didn't want.

Lessons, however, are the juicy moments of life. By *juicy* I mean we get tested. Falling in love is a test. Winning the lottery is a test. So is the death of someone you love, or homelessness. We all get at least one major life lesson or test, but usually more. If you think about your life, you can probably tease out three or four themes of what it's been about so far. Roads you've traveled, detours. A good astrologer could take your life story and map out the transits using your joys and sorrows as a compass.

My Astro Routine

For years I've used a spiral-bound astrological planner. It tells me what's going on in the sky each day, in list form, and uses glyphs for the planets and signs instead of words. Don't let this intimidate you though. Many astrological planners have glossaries so you can learn a thing or two while keeping track of the daily sky.

For example, you can turn to any day of the week and see which planets are prominent that day and which ones aren't. Every day is different. What's the Moon doing? What's Mercury up to? Did something go retrograde? The glossary will tell you what the Sun, Moon, or Mercury means in astrology, and so on. You won't learn everything from an astrology planner, but it's an excellent place to start.

I also regularly use an app to see if the planets are interacting with my *own* birth chart at any given time and what it might mean (whether or not I agree with the interpretation!).

𝒫LEASE 𝑅EMEMBER

We are dealing with two separate things: the sky itself versus what the sky is doing to you.

Familiarize yourself with the glyphs and basic astrology terms, but please don't feel bad if it takes time to grasp. There are some glyphs that I still haven't committed to memory, although there really are a finite number of items you need for understanding the daily sky or your own astrology, which is why I like the astrology planners. They give the meat of the matter and leave out the superfluous.

The internet is your friend, although astrology has gotten so popular it can be hard for beginners to navigate the sea of apps and sites. Also, big names aren't always the best. I recommend doing general internet searches for topics and terms you are curious about and go from there. Don't just stop at the first, second, or third page of a search. You can also ask astrologers on social media for their favorite sites and resources.

Think about how you might like to get your astrology info (which is something we talked about in the previous chapter). A paper calendar? A phone app? Professional software? Friendly blogs? YouTubers? It wasn't until I was writing this chapter that I realized I like my astrology delivered over multiple mediums. I regularly visit an app, my planner, a couple of YouTube astrologers, plus a free website for client charts because I like how the charts look. And I'm probably forgetting a few.

TRACKING THE DAILY SKY

If you are starting to learn astrology on your own or want to start tracking the daily sky on a regular basis, here is what I most recommend:

Get thyself an astrological planner and look at it each day.

Review that day's stars while drinking your morning beverage or before you head to work. What kind of day does it look like? Is it mostly neutral? Positive? Edgy? Your astrology glossary will help you figure this out or you can go straight to the web and dig.

It's not enough to know that the Sun is trine Jupiter that day. You want to know what each of those words mean. It's like Dinah Washington's song "What a Difference a Day Makes." Again, look online or use the planner itself for unfamiliar terms.

ASTROLOGY IS BREAD

The suggestions here can help you quickly get to know the language of astrology, although they aren't a substitute for deeper learning. It's like buying bread at the store versus baking it yourself. Sure it's easy and convenient to buy a loaf of bread. You're hungry and you need to eat. The bread is there. But maybe that loaf, either because you love it or hate it, will inspire you to bake your own. If you bake your own, you get to experience an earthy, sensual process that will make your kitchen smell like love. Astrology, my friends, is bread.

WHAT HAPPENED NEXT

I'm back at the Magic Cafe as I write to you and thinking about the story I told you earlier, the one about the astrologer and the talking birth chart. What happened next was that she closed her big black notebook and left the room in a dazed panic. Although she'd been engaged in the mystical arts for many years, and likely many lifetimes, nothing like this had *ever* happened to her before.

To be continued.

EVERYBODY LOVES THE MOON.

Falling in Love with the Moon

I never paid much attention to the moon, besides memories of being a little one in the back seat of my parents' station wagon and thinking the moon was following us. I know that the moon is a big deal, what with all those phases and new moons and full moons and eclipses. There are entire religions, like my own Jewish one, that follow not a solar calendar but a lunar one.

It wasn't until I fell in love with astrology that I fell in love with Her Majesty, the moon, which is associated, in astrology, with mothers, women, family, food, memory, home, our feelings, our needs, safety, security, habits, instincts.

Moon as Memory Lane

Years ago, when I was learning astrology, our teacher had a habit of using the current sky as examples for us. Say there was a New Moon in Virgo that week. On the dry-erase board, he would draw a huge chart of the current sky and put in all the planets one by one for the exact moment of the New Moon.

He would then choose a lucky student, or more if the class was small that day, and compare the New Moon chart to our charts. It was so magical. What did it all mean?

In the brand of personal astrology that I do, New Moons symbolize something new in your life, a beginning, and Full Moons represent an ending or a culmination, sometimes a revelation. New Moon is the seed. Full Moon is what has grown. The time of the New Moon is dark. Look up and you will see a swath of endless sky, dotted with stars. Compare this with your average bright, voluptuous Full Moon who hides nothing. Secrets come out!

In astrology land (and no doubt in other lands too), we talk about "setting intentions" on New Moons and even Full Moons. Setting intentions is like making a wish. Something you hope for. Something you plan for. Something you want very much. If you're smart, you focus all your attention and energy and desire on the wish. *This is the essence of magic.*

The actual New Moon and Full Moon days are thus a special time, usually happening twice a month, when you can take a break from the quotidian, have a mini retreat, and think about your life, aka, calm the hell down.

My thinking about the moon hasn't really changed since those early years of learning astrology. I still look for the coming New Moon and Full Moon in my birth chart each month, wondering what will be, making predictions for myself and others. We are all that baby in the back seat being followed by the mysterious moon.

Big Moon, Big Eclipse

Eclipses are New or Full Moons, but superpotent ones from an astrological perspective. They don't happen every month but usually in twos or threes at least twice a year. They are more radical, revolutionary, and life-changing than a typical New or Full Moon, which can come and go without your noticing. It's like a minor holiday compared to a major one. In America, Thanksgiving is a major holiday (a time for family get-togethers and shopping due to the famous Black Friday sales) versus, say, Flag Day. (What is Flag Day anyway?)

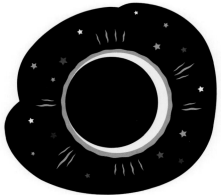

Eclipses, like the other lunations, are occasions to stop, slow down, and think about our lives. With an eclipse, however, there's an emphasis on bigger time frames, the next three months, six months, year ahead. In my own experience, personally and with students, I have seen eclipses commence great change, from the chaotic to the effervescent.

••• 𝕳OMEWORK •••

A LITTLE MOON MAGIC:
TAROT SPREADS FOR NEW & FULL MOONS

I created a few moony tarot spreads for you, but first, a few recommendations:

Do these tarot spreads within twenty-four hours of any New Moon or Full Moon (Eclipses included).

Do them after sundown (if possible), but any convenient time when you aren't feeling rushed is good. Remember to inhale, exhale.

You don't have to use a tarot deck. Use any pictorial or oracle or animal deck.

Do these spreads with other rituals or do them alone.

Do them just once or more than once, but keep track of your cards in your tarot journal. Keep track of how you feel when the cards show their faces.

Do them with your tarot friend or do them alone.

Lay out the cards any way you please. If desired, you can add an additional card at any time. Folks often do this when they feel puzzled by what a card might be saying. Just know that sometimes more cards doesn't mean more clarity.

Tarot for the New Moon (One Card)

Where should I put my energy this month?

Tarot for a New Moon Eclipse (One Card)

Where should I put my energy this year?

Tarot for the New Moon or New Moon Eclipse (Six Cards)

What do I need to begin?

How do I begin it?

Guidance from above.

Next steps.

How am I doing?

What will bring me peace of mind?

Tarot for the Full Moon (One Card)

What should I release this month?

Tarot for a Full Moon Eclipse (One Card)

What should I release this year?

Tarot for the Full Moon or Full Moon Eclipse (Six Cards)

What needs to be let go from my life? (Alternate: What is culminating in my life?)

What needs to be kept but transformed in my life? (Alternate: How do I handle the coming changes?)

Guidance from above.

Next steps.

How am I doing?

What will bring me peace of mind?

Additional Tarot Questions for New Moons or Full Moons

Pull cards for any of these questions, either as stand-alone spreads or add them to the ones above:

What do I need to make me feel safe?

Show me my true home / what I need to feel at home.

Show the meaning of this New / Full Moon for me personally.

It Could Happen to You

When we last left our astrologer, she had run out of her room, alarmed by the talking chart. It was a full month later, after midnight, in the wee hours, so I'm told, that she returned to her workroom to discover her big black book, which contained all her copious notations and glyphs and graphs and potions and calculations and formulas … had vanished.

MORE GOOD ASTROLOGY HABITS FOR STAR LOVERS.

How to Succeed at Astrology: Good Habits for Current and Future Star Lovers

Dear star lovers, I want to give you a few suggestions now for good astrology habits, using the first eleven cards of the tarot as a template and guide. The Rider-Waite-Smith deck was my inspiration here, from the Fool through the Wheel of Fortune.

Why astrology and tarot together? If you decide to include them in your collection of cool stuff, you'll discover how well they complement each other while expanding your intuition. Also, right now is a perfect opportunity to do a little more tarot talk (although if you ask me it's never a bad time to add a card or two).

The Fool

The Fool is bold. The Fool is brave. The Fool is a little impulsive. The Fool loves something new, striking out on a fresh path, a wild beginning. I recommend to you this Fool mindset as you start (or continue) your astrology studies. Have an open mind and a beginner's heart. Let the star path show you its twists and turns as you enter this world without any preconceived notions.

Let's say you're an intermediate astrology student. Maybe an almost-expert. The truth is even experts start over. Forget everything you know, just like the Fool does. Embark on your astrology journey as if all the highways are new, the car is new, even the sky and stars are brand-new, just for you, as you look up at them for the first time. Let yourself *begin*.

THE MAGICIAN

The Magician is confident. The Magician is clever. The Magician is a master. I recommend you pick an area of astrology, a part that calls to you, and commit to it. Don't worry about understanding all of astrology. No one does. Aim for becoming a specialist, like a good scholar. Discover what part of astrology delights you the most. Let it obsess you. You can always branch out later. You no doubt will.

Maybe it's a deep understanding of the signs. Perhaps it's how to predict the future using ancient techniques. What I'm talking about here isn't just talent but prowess born of deep focus.

What skills do you need? The Magician might say you have to use your brain (the suit of Swords) and your heart (the suit of Cups), and be practical about it (the Pentacles suit), but also inspired and passionate (Wands). Approach astrology with your entire self.

THE HIGH PRIESTESS

The High Priestess is mysterious, quiet, intuitive. She knows how to keep things hidden. You don't have to tell anybody what you're doing (your choice), but I do recommend you keep at least some of your astrology work under wraps while it weaves its way into your life. Let it be your secret companion for a little while.

Try doing your astrology work in the dark of night, under a New Moon. Do it by candlelight. Unlike the Magician who labors, the High Priestess receives wisdom just by opening her hands. She knows that the stars and heavens will speak.

I also recommend you include tranquil time with your astrology work. Let's say you spend two hours with a complex book or drawing a chart by hand and your mind gets weary. Make sure to let the information sit and be still. The High Priestess would.

The Empress

The Empress is passionate, creative, beautiful. She's always birthing something. The Empress says, "I have it." Life is not just fine, but abundant. I recommend your astrology work be the work of pleasure. Don't do it unless you enjoy it. This is when you'll know for sure whether astrology is part of your spiritual path. Use pleasure as your measure. Do you love it? Is it beautiful to you?

Sure, you can study astrology on the fly, in a rush, but the Empress would recommend you feel relaxed when you open those books, feet up, dressed comfortably, a glass of wine (or other favorite drink) in your hand. Even though I've been using the phrase astrology *work*, it shouldn't be a chore. Astrologers send love letters to the stars. The Empress would, too, I think, in flowing cursive handwriting.

The Emperor

The Emperor can be rigid, it's true. He balances the Empress's sensual nature. He's not about pleasure, but structures and rules. Structures and rules are a theme around here, that practice makes … practice.

I recommend you follow the Emperor and create an orderly course of study for yourself. Set aside a regular time to learn your personal astrology. Have a weekly session just for current transits. Keep track of the New and Full Moons. Decide on a schedule and stick to it.

The Emperor, also, is a leader. When I think of your astrology work through this particular tarot-card lens, I see you teaching a class on how to read the cards and stars. Sound good? When I was learning astrology, I never ever thought I would be reading charts for others, much less teaching it. But here we are. This may also be your fate.

The Hierophant

The Hierophant is a traditional kind of guy, large and in charge, and has a similar vibe to the Emperor, liking structure and rules—but he's also akin to the contemplative High Priestess. He knows things. Spiritual teaching is his gift.

The study of astrology isn't merely divination (which is an awesome thing in and of itself) or a tool for self-growth, but a mystical pathway. You can turn away from this path, or never step foot on it at all, but please realize what astrology is: passage to another world. Study of it will take you there.

I've often said (about astrology *and* tarot) I don't know how it works—I just know that it does. With the Hierophant comes this recommendation: make sure your learning is solid, not soggy. Learn the firm foundations. Study the planets. Study the signs. Start there.

The Lovers

The Lovers are happy and naked. The Lovers are blessed by an angel. Now, I'm not necessarily promoting naked tarot (although be my guest), but I do recommend having an astrology friend just as you acquired a tarot friend (see "Tarot Will Make You Psychic"). It can be the same friend or a different one. Why? So that you have someone to discuss astrology with!

Don't learn this awesome stuff alone. You are going to want to talk about it. With people. Trust me. This can be through a real-life group or online. It can be small or big or one-on-one. You could even find a favorite podcast where you call in like an obsessive fan. Like the Lovers card, I recommend that you find like-minded souls so you can compare your natal charts, track your transits together, and share the love.

The Chariot

The Chariot is victorious, but there are bumps in the road, starts and stops. There will be times when you need to get out of the car and stretch your legs. There will be times when you don't want to ask *anyone* if they know their Sun, Moon, and Ascendent, and you let your astrology obsession rest. On other days, you'll be begging to run the birth chart of everyone in the room.

There are always detours along the way, no matter what we discover on the spiritual path. Sometimes you'll be all fired up, and other times want to forget it all. You may even want to push the damn Chariot into the ocean. It's normal.

Approach your astrology work like the Chariot: getting lost is part of the trip, but ultimately you will reach your destination (and then the one after that, and the one after that).

STRENGTH

Strength is gentle, slow to anger, unyielding. Be gentle with yourself, please, as you consider adding astrology to your life. Learning astrology will take time, so go one step at a time. Although I'm going to suggest you read widely and often, and immerse yourself in the waters of the stars, Strength recommends a soft pace.

If you start to feel frustrated or overwhelmed, take breaks but don't quit. These days we have blogs and sites and apps, in addition to good books and teachers. Yes, there's a ton of information out there. You'll find the perfect book, perfect teacher, other resources. Go slow.

Many versions of this card feature a woman and a lion. Is she closing the lion's jaws or comforting him? Maybe both. In my favorite deck, she looks positively serene. The road may seem everlasting at times, but it's worth traveling.

The Hermit

The Hermit is alone in the near dark. The Hermit moves slowly. The Hermit is the light of wisdom. Often depicted holding a lantern, it's serious solitude when the Hermit arises in your head or your tarot spread. Time for quiet, time for study, and not unlike the High Priestess, but the emphasis here is on knowledge recovered and discovered, not merely known or intuited.

With the Hermit comes this recommendation: read, read, read. Build an occult library of your own with real, touchable books, not just electronic ones. Return to the habit of lovely covers and printed ink and books that get wet in the rain. You don't need thousands. Shoot for at least twenty-five in your astrology collection! *The more books, the more wisdom* could be the Hermit's motto, who not only reads but studies and, yes, teaches what she learns.

WHEEL OF FORTUNE

The Wheel of Fortune is unpredictable. The Wheel goes round and round. The Wheel is often good, albeit unexpected, progress for you. With the Wheel comes this recommendation: study astrology without expectation.

See where it takes you. Let it lead you. Be wild and free with the crazy stars. Let those Emperor and Hierophant and Magician good habits that we talked about mix and meld with the adventuresome Chariot and Fool.

The Wheel of Fortune is associated with fate. You chose this book. You chose to be here. When the Wheel of Fortune comes to visit, please understand that the map of your journey has disappeared, and the car has a mind of its own. Maybe you'll pick astrology up and drop it. Maybe you'll study it for life. And maybe you'll be the next great astrology writer and thinker. Trust, my dear star lovers. Trust the Wheel of fate.

SOON WE MUST LEAVE
ASTROLOGY LAND.
A FEW MORE THOUGHTS, THEN BACK
OUT ON THE ROAD.

Dear Star Lovers, Don't Be Afraid of the Dark

After a full day of rain, we have sunshine today in the big city, and one good sweater is warm enough. It's Monday and I'm back at the Magic Cafe, thinking of how to tie it all together for you, this astrology thing.

Obviously, I love astrology. But will it suit you? What do the cards say? Pull three.

··· HOMEWORK ···

IS IT LOVE? TAROT SPREAD

This is a three-card spread. Shuffle and get ready to draw. The first card is you. Put it to the left. The second card represents astrology. Put it to the right. Then lay down a card between those two. That one is the energy, the relationship between you and astrology. That card will tell you almost everything.

Worry not if it's an intense card, a serious card, a disruptive card, if the images disturb you. To help soothe any tarot anxiety, return to your books (or favorite search engine) and discover deeply what each card of this little tarot spread means.

All the better, I think, if they *are* intense, serious, and even disruptive cards. We are talking about our spiritual life in here, and it, like the truth, isn't always pretty. Don't be afraid of the dark.

Pull one more card now. This one will represent what astrology *should* be for you, your life, your spiritual path.

Astro Reminders and a Story About Shame

It's easy to learn the basics. Please learn the basics. I can't emphasize this enough. In the previous chapters, I walked you through what to learn first and how to learn it—for a solid astrological foundation. Enough to get you started and more. And here is the why, as in why learn astrology: It is the *best* for understanding yourself. It is the *best* for understanding others. It is the *best* for making sense of your place in the universe.

Remember that story I told you in "Instructions for the Star Road"? It was about an astrology reading I had years ago. My teacher was analyzing my birth chart, and he singled out this one thing. *One. Thing.* The reading could have ended right then and there. All of us have a showstopper or two in our birth chart. Something that explains almost everything about us. He immediately found mine.

Once I knew what this map of me had to say, I stopped feeling so ashamed. Why shame? All my life I was told that I felt too much, was too sensitive, too intense. He was talking about the parts of me that others devalued, discarded. *You mean it's not my fault? These strong emotions are just … who I am?*

Astrology can give you this. It can give you back your soul, your center, your peace, your sense of who you are, make you proud of who you are.

Now for you it may be something else. For you it may not be emotional intensity, but ambition so terrifying you can think of nothing else but changing the world. Or you may go in and out of dramatic romantic relationships so fast that no one can keep track, including you. You wonder if there's something wrong with you, but you are probably just living your astrology and need help in how to turn pain into gold. It can be done, star lovers. This is what astrology is for.

ONE CAUTION FOR THE ROAD

I want to give you one warning now about the study of astrology. *Please do not use it to freak yourself out.*

If you use astrology for making predictions, even simple ones, like how a New Moon may manifest for you, there will be times when you feel you should have stayed in bed and ignored the stars entirely. The same goes for listening to or reading too much astrology content that relies on scare-tactic tones. You know the kind I mean. Mercury goes retrograde (which it does three times a year at least) and the anxious astro lovers amp up the doom and gloom.

The internet now churns out spiritual teachers, astrologers, gurus, and card readers daily. Not everyone is worth listening to and some can be downright baneful or just plain wrong.

Another way this can play out: Every now and then I get a student who wants me to look at their transits and tell them about the bad stuff on the way. Not just an honest assessment but spooky dangers ahead. I also know readers who seem to specialize in "warning" type readings. Beware of this person. Beware of that day. Now, if someone asks me is this a good day to launch a business or have an operation, I'll give them an honest answer, based on my astrological findings. But the warning I have for you here is to beware of folks who peddle in such styles.

The astrology I know and love is here to empower you, teach you, soothe you, help you, understand you—not to make your days harder or filled with fear. We've got enough of those *without* astrology!

Yes, it's helpful to know when an upcoming transit is difficult and dark and how long it will last and how it may play out in your life—but that's reality, not grim intimidation masquerading as divination.

OUR CONTINUING STORY

Let us return now to the ancient astrologer you met a few chapters ago. A full month had passed before she returned to her workroom to discover that her huge book of glyphs and graphs and notations and potions had disappeared.

But where *did* she go? A month is not a minute. She must have gone somewhere.

Legend has it that by morning light, the book reappeared, and not wide open upon her table, where she left it, but neatly placed on one of her many bookshelves. Strange.

Legend also tells us that the chart continued to speak and not only that chart, but all the ones that followed when she drew them by hand. In fact, rumors swirled of raucous parties (even the neighbors complained), but how could that be? She lived alone and kept to herself like a hardworking witch. It's a mystery to this very day.

If you include astrology in your collection of cool stuff, will this happen for you? Will your charts talk and dance? Only one way to find out.

NEXT STOP

NOW IT'S TIME TO MEET THE INVISIBLE WORLD.

ℛECOMMENDATIONS:
ℐN ℳy Astrology Suitcase

Llewellyn's Daily Planetary Guide is my go-to astrology calendar/planner. I use it every day! And I'm not just saying that because Llewellyn is my publisher. The daily guide will show you what the planets are up to and also has definitions of key terms. Perfect for all levels, especially for those who want more paper in their life and less tech (apps/software).

The tech: TimePassages and Astro Gold are two phone apps I'm familiar with. This topic is a slippery slope because how good an app is may depend on your astrology knowledge and what you're using it for. Also, I'm old-school and no doubt there are newer options touted as the latest and greatest. You'll have to explore the app store on your phone and see for yourself. You can always download and then uninstall if an app doesn't fit your needs.

Like a good astrology calendar, both these apps define crucial astrological terms (good for beginners), and you can also create charts (good for everyone). Each app has its limits or quirks, but I don't mind. I just like to know, on the go, where the planets are, what they're doing to me. I particularly like the Astro Gold "Reports" section, where you can get a nice long list of your (or someone else's) transits (plus explanations if you want them).

> **ᏢLEASE NOTE:** an app won't always distinguish between what I consider important astrology details versus what I see as less important. Also, sometimes apps will give too much information, which can be unnecessarily confusing or annoying.

So why am I even recommending them? Astrology apps are useful, helpful tools. They can help you learn astrology, and it's nice to have one, or two, in the palm of your hand. Apps can't replace a good teacher or a great book, but for looking up a chart on the go, it's what you want. Otherwise, how else will you see into the soul of your new love muffin? We need that chart and we need it now!

For websites, some of the same logic applies. Astrology is everywhere online, but when I was starting out, **Astrodienst** and **Cafe Astrology** were the gold standard and pretty much all we had at the time. Both sites have tons of information (more than either of the apps I mention above), great for those seeking to learn or review astrology, no matter their experience level. And of course, as I mentioned earlier in this section, you can always do an online search of any astrological phrase you think up, no matter how weird or obscure or popular. The internet will offer dozens of entries. How can you separate the helpful from the useless? You'll figure that out the more you learn.

My own site, **MoonPluto Astrology,** isn't encyclopedic in terms of information like the two I mention above, but more personal. I would tell stories about my own life, including how hard transits were affecting me (and most likely you too). I would blog about my astrology obsessions, whatever they were at the time, and give advice. I was always giving advice. I don't blog as much as I used to (the site's been around since 2011), but clients and students still tell me it's how they first found me, from the blog.

Books

Rex E. Bills's *The Rulership Book* is literally an astrological book of lists, divided by sign and planet and house. Read Bills and you'll learn that Mercury rules memorandums, Aquarius rules idealists, and the Fourth House rules crops. And more, so much more.

Isabel Hickey's *Astrology: A Cosmic Science.* This one is unlike any astrology book I've ever read. Her writing is so clear and yet philosophical. Cosmic! I return to Hickey when I need to feel reinspired and especially love her keyword lists.

Howard Sasportas's *The Twelve Houses* is another deep one. Sasportas is spiritual, psychological, and a good writer—everything I love in a book.

Finally, there's my first book, *The Little Book of Saturn*. It's a solid introduction to astrology but focuses mostly on, you guessed it, Saturn! It can help you with your own (and your loved ones') Saturn problems, which is something Saturn loves to do: test us and cause problems!

Authors

I recommend these authors, although I haven't read all their books:

Steven Forrest • Donna Cunningham

Linda Goodman • Tracy Marks

Robert Hand • Demetra George

Caroline W. Casey, • Stephen Arroyo

Marion D. March • Joan McEvers

and any book that Howard Sasportas

and Liz Greene wrote together.

So You Want an Astrology Reading— Who to Trust?

My advice: trust how you feel. Maybe you're on a social media platform and reading a blog post or watching a video and you get that kindred-soul feeling, that this person might be able to help you or understand you. Pay attention to that. It's real.

There's no law that says you have to get readings, but it can be a great way to learn astrology. Pay attention to not only what the astrologer is saying but *how* they say it, how they put things together. Ask them questions. It's a great way to learn.

ℐF ℐ ℋAD TO ℭHOOSE

I know it's a lot. Probably the biggest suitcase in the book. If I had to pick *only* two things I'd say grab a copy of **March and McEvers's** *The Only Way to Learn Astrology (Volume 1)* and get *Llewellyn's Planetary Guide*, and that's your two-book starter kit right there. Then call me when the going gets tough.

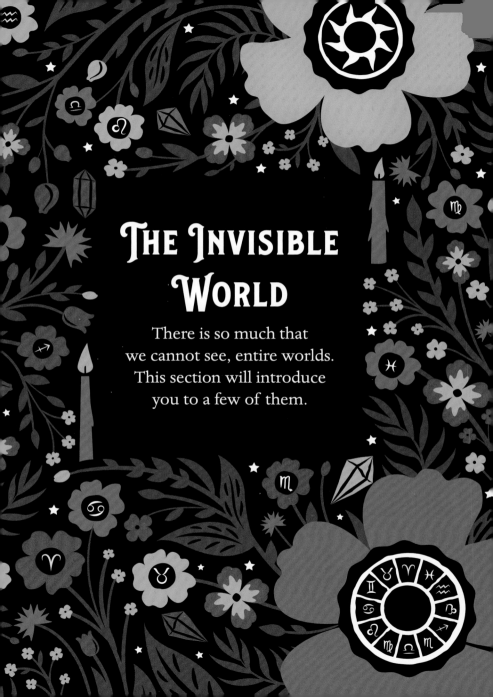

The Invisible World

There is so much that
we cannot see, entire worlds.
This section will introduce
you to a few of them.

The Accidental Medium

The other morning, I was having coffee with a friend. We hadn't seen each other in years. He started to tell me a story, all the while telling me that he didn't believe in "spooky stuff," as he called it.

It was the story of a dear friend of his who had recently passed away and how this friend often wore a top hat. One night, not long after that friend died, he and another friend were at a bar, in Brooklyn, and they saw a man in a top hat. It wasn't Halloween. When he and his companion were heading home, by subway, they saw two more men—both in top hats.

My friend ended his story by saying to me: "This is what people would call a sign, right? But I don't believe in signs." Yet, he also noted how interesting it was that not long after the death of this friend, the top-hat lover, to have multiple top-hat sightings in one night! But, no, not a sign. Of course not.

Signs

We usually think of mediums as those who initiate communication with the dead, but here was my friend, just out and about, living his life, and definitely getting what I would call a sign. He knew enough about this stuff to know that others might find it significant too.

I would also say you picking up this book is a sign. Turning to this section right away, a sign. Reading this chapter? Definitely a sign. I believe in signs, but I am exaggerating here to make a point.

You, my friend, are not crazy-nuts for finding meaning in the stuff that others don't, which often is the stuff that others are afraid of, or don't understand, or just dismiss out of hand. My friend was telling me a supernatural story and denying that's what it was. Three top hats in one night? Just a coincidence?

Like with all the stories in this book, I'm not here to pressure you. What I want is to share with you what I know, give you suggestions for realms to explore that could belong in your collection of cool stuff, your spiritual path. Mediumship may be one of those realms.

ARE YOU AN ACCIDENTAL MEDIUM TOO?

My friend was an accidental medium that night. You may be one as well.

A story: One day a different friend asked me if I could bring back a message for them from a dear departed relative. I can't remember exactly what I did first, if I pulled any tarot cards, or concentrated real hard, or not at all. Concentrating "not at all" is what I call "tuning in"—letting the mind go blank and lose focus.

I do, however, remember that the process of receiving information, the way the information came to me, didn't feel that different from working with the tarot—and yet it did. It was more visual than usual, and I immediately started to feel warm all over. I felt something that I would call love, felt enveloped by it, as I began to tell my friend what I was seeing, which was her son dancing around her, letting her know he was okay. I was picking up on some of his mannerisms and jokes, silly ways he would act when he was here in a body. And also that now he was fine. No pain.

If you are an accidental medium, you may experience such things and not know what it is because you never thought to ask: Is this the dead?

Death Is Not the End

Here is something many believe (and many don't), and I ask you to consider it: that death is not the end. There is a part of you (soul or spirit) that doesn't ever die. Your loved ones, people and animals, are still here, but in a different form. Communication with them is entirely possible. Yes, they may send signs. Yes, you can talk to them. Yes, they can talk to you. One of the most important things that will come up over and over in this book is *trust*, trusting your perceptions, trusting what you experience.

As I started to answer more and more questions for folks about the dead, I realized it wasn't always the same. Sometimes I didn't feel enveloped by love, although I often did. Sometimes the departed stood back a little or didn't want to talk. As I talked to more of them, I noticed more variation. Sometimes the messages were muddy. Other times the details were spot-on: Yes, he was a heavy smoker. Yes, he was short. Yes, he loved that dog, and they went for endless car rides in the summer in Los Angeles, especially in 1972.

Loss as a Gateway

I lost my parents decades ago. Both died when I was in my twenties. Looking back, I'm not sure how I survived such a break, such a reality shift, and I'm not sure I did. I probably became a ghost then, too, at least for a little while.

If you think back, you can probably pinpoint times in your own life like that, and they don't have to be trauma or loss, but they may be. Something shocked you into a new reality, the way those paddles on medical television shows bring critical patients back to life and a steady heart rhythm. Who do you become after such times? The path changes irretrievably. Something happened to your soul then. You received a gift, or a coupon for a gift, that you couldn't redeem until years after the fact, perhaps a talent for mediumship or psychic ability, or a passion for the Invisible World.

You don't have to know exactly what happens after we die to talk to the dead, to become a medium. You don't have to understand. There's really no job requirement. And, honestly, it's not that different from any other kind of "psychic work" or intuitive messaging.

For example, if you start playing around with astrology and tarot and making predictions using either tool, you'll find that mediumship isn't such a leap. We're stirring the same cauldron here. It's the same sea.

On the other hand, you may find a special calling to work with the dead or that communicating with them is stronger for you than any other spiritual task. All I ask is that you begin to explore and consider whether the Invisible World is where you belong. Maybe you already do. (I can see you nodding your head as I write these words.) In a future chapter of this section, I'll give you some instructions.

The Call of the Dead

Why would any sane person *want* to become a medium? Because you miss your loved ones. Because you don't and want to find out why. Because *they* talk to you, and it's about time you answered back. There's no right reason. I think many folks just feel a calling. Some of us just want to walk between worlds.

LET'S MEET THE SPIRIT GUIDES.

A Quick Guide to Spirit Guides

The streets of Brooklyn are haunted and I don't mean by ghosts. What I mean is that I feel the presence of the invisible, in every bodega, every park, every pizza joint. You may feel this way about your own town, that you're acquainted with the spirit life there, the *spirit guides* of that place.

If you have any interest in metaphysical topics at all, you've probably heard this phrase *spirit guide*. What does it mean?

I can't remember the first time I heard the phrase. It may have been in a book by famous psychic Sylvia Browne. I had one or two of her books over the years, long before I learned astrology and got into psychic stuff myself.

For our purposes here, consider a spirit guide an entity or being who doesn't currently inhabit a physical body, and maybe they never did.

A Note on Safety

Please note that not all entities or beings (who don't currently inhabit a physical body and maybe never did) are good, just like not all humans are good. Some are mischievous, or lawless, or downright destructive. But I wouldn't call a meddling presence a "spirit guide" anyway. I'd call them something else.

My truth: when I sit down to talk to the dead or I am seeking spirit *guidance*, I'm not overly worried that I may pick up a bad one, some less-than savory type hitchhiking along the astral plane who got caught up in my New Moon intention net, for example. Just like when I pray (and I grew up praying in a traditional Jewish way, which isn't overly concerned with bad vibes), I'm not worried that a demon might intercept my prayer. It's just not my worldview or belief.

I believe you're more likely to try to contact dead Uncle Dale and get dead Uncle Eddie coming forward—rather than a troubled "spirit guide" wanting to mess with you—although it really depends on you, your worldview, your belief, your personality, your spiritual practices, your fate. We're all different! Do confused or malevolent entities exist? Many believe so, but that's not what I'm talking about here.

Also, if seeking communication with the Invisible World makes you uncomfortable, then by all means don't do it. Trust yourself.

THE SPIRIT OF ANTARCTICA

Now, I like the term *spirit guide* because it's familiar to many of us, and it's general enough and bland enough to fold into the various categories. When I use the phrase, I do mean a spirit who is benevolent, wise. Neutral at worst. For me, spirit guides are wondrous supernatural beings whose purpose is to help us. Sounds too good to be true, I know, but I believe in magic.

A spirit guide could be your recently deceased relative or long ago ancestor or archangel from the Old Testament or an animal or…something you can't describe at all because you do not have the words and you don't know what "it" is. You may feel guided by the rain. You may feel guided by Antarctica. You may feel guided by the coffee shop you inhabit every day around 8:00 a.m., and that coffee shop, just like you, has a spirit, a soul.

These guides are here to help us. They have thoughts, or feelings, or actions, or all of the above. They have guidance, obviously, and information, like the tarot cards that come to life, but better. They are real, like you and me, and yet beyond us.

Partly Cloudy With a Chance of Archangel Michael

Sometimes my friends or students will ask me for messages from their guides or ask who their guides are. They want to know something, anything. Who is around me? What can they tell me? Humans, clearly, aren't enough for us, and this is okay. It's okay to want to feel less alone, feel purpose and continuity in our lives. One way to get it is through these connections to the Invisible World. Spirit guides know things that we don't. Also, sometimes our problems feel too big for human hands.

In the world I live in (the world of astrologers, tarot readers, psychics, Witches, etc.) talking about spirit guides (and you might use different words to describe the same thing) is as common as talking about the weather. No big deal for us—rain on Monday, snow on Tuesday, partly cloudy Wednesday—but you know there are people in your family or community who might look at you funny if you started talking about what your guides said to you last night and how Archangel Michael protected you while you were on the subway. Once upon a time, I thought I was too sophisticated for spirit guides, that it was some empty new age phrase. I was wrong though. Sometimes simple words are exactly what's needed to talk about the magic all around us.

It's Like the Sky

Why try to talk to spirit guides at all? Why seek them out? Because they have answers. And because you have questions. And these don't have to be dark-night-of-the-soul type questions. It can be anytime, any topic. You can talk to them when you're feeling good. You can thank them for being there. You can ask them who they are. You can ask them where they are. You can be in the mood for searching. And you can definitely talk to them when you are wrestling with the hard questions of life: why you're here and why bother. You can ring them in your angst and in your gratefulness. And no, you won't be bothering them at all.

Also, it's a common human desire to try to make sense of death, of our suffering, to wonder if there's a god or higher power roaming around, in charge of us, looking after us. This is one reason why getting to know the Invisible World could be a good thing. You get a team.

Sometimes I would wonder if spirit guides really do exist. Other times I'm certain of it. Imagine if we lived our lives this way, all the time—*that we are never not connected*. It's like forgetting to look up at the sky. We just have to remember it's there.

How to Reach Out

There is a foundation to all this spiritual work that doesn't change, and its themes run through all the chapters in this section. That foundation is being able to quiet your mind, even for just a little while. Not silence your mind and shut it tight, but shush it a little. Later in the book, I will give you some specific meditation instruction that can help with this. It's one of the best things you can do for any spiritual or magical practice.

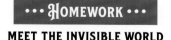

MEET THE INVISIBLE WORLD

Are you ready to talk to the Invisible World? Try this.

Ambitious Method

Set aside fifteen minutes any time of day when you have some quiet in your surroundings and can sit undisturbed.

Set an intention that you are ready to receive information about spirit guides who are around you. Set an intention that the information may come through any of your senses, including smell and taste.

Your spirit guide may tell you about a favorite food, for example, and you may smell it before you know what it is.

Do this every day—yes, every day—for a full month.

Keep your journal and pen nearby to write down any images or thoughts—anything at all that comes to mind or that your senses pick up.

And if you get nothing, you can write that down too. The main thing is to keep a record of whatever you are perceiving, seeing, hearing, knowing. Do this consistently, fifteen minutes each day. Write it all down, even if it doesn't make sense at the time.

Basically, you are sitting and waiting and making space for the guides to come through.

Try not to worry if you don't get anything right away. Try not to worry if you get all kinds of visions populated with beings you don't understand. Just go back day after day to your sitting place.

It will be interesting to discover who shows up, how long it takes, how chatty they are, what changes day to day.

Quick Method

Use your tarot cards. I recommend a simple spread. Just one card.

Ask the cards to show you an important spirit guide who is around you. Even if you don't feel it, believe what you are being told or shown. That this *person* is nearby and is yours.

Don't rely only on your own intuition for knowing what the card is trying to tell you. Consult your personal tarot library for additional meanings.

Write it all down, of course, in your journal. You did get a journal, right?

A STORY ABOUT A SHAMAN.

Young Shaman & Other Spirit–Guide Stories

Some years ago, I fortuitously found a young man on the internet (haven't we all?) who was advertising his spiritual services. He seemed like the real deal to me, and I was in an exploratory phase. He called himself a shaman, and I purchased a short email reading from him.

I wanted to learn everything under the sun in those days, including Wicca, Witchcraft, Hoodoo, Voodoo, shamanism, and all manner of magic.

He also lived in Brooklyn, so I scheduled a shamanic journey with him. I'll never forget how he lay on the floor that day with headphones on as he went into a light trance. I could hear the faint sound of drums as he went out of "this world" and into another. Throughout the journey, he would ask various entities for assistance.

Some of the names of these entities I recognized, as they were famous gods or goddesses or angels. I was hearing a story unfold as it happened, but it was my story. He was journeying with a question we came up with together, in search of an answer. I don't presume to say he would call those entities "spirit guides," but it fits my definition for sure.

I do not claim to be a shaman, but after that day, I started going into trance states on my own, to search for answers, and I realized, too, that it was something I'd been doing all along when I meditated. I just didn't have a context for it. It didn't have a name.

••• ℌOMEWORK •••

HOW TO CULTIVATE YOUR SPIRIT GUIDES
BECAUSE THEY, TOO, ARE A GARDEN

You can try to find out who your guides are by following any of the techniques and homework suggestions in this section. You can talk to them, including asking for help or guidance. They love that. You can give them gifts. You can establish special places in your home that are dedicated to them.

You can also create an altar, which is most definitely a special place (more about altars in "Real-Life Magic"). There are many books available (or do an online search) that discuss what gifts (like food or drink or flowers or other items) particular famous gods, goddesses, saints, or guides enjoy. You may also want to ask *your* spirit guides directly what they prefer. You can put these items on the altar, light a candle there, and talk to your guides on a New Moon or Full Moon. These are special days. You can also ditch all ceremony and chat with them whenever you want, however you want, no gift or poetic words required. I know that some folks, however, prefer a more formal approach.

If Elijah the prophet were one of my spirit guides, I might put a glass of wine on the altar for him, as we do on the festival of Passover. If a desert god like Set were one of my guides, I might include sand to make him feel at home. If Bast were a guide, perhaps a ceramic cat would find its way home to me.

More Ideas

Hang up pictures of your spirit guides, what they look like or what you feel they look like. Adorn yourself with reminders of them. Devote special times of the day/week/month for talking to them. Set a place for them at the table.

Let's say rose quartz is one of your spirit guides. Yes, even an object can be a guide for you. Some people are very connected to crystals (I know a few of them myself). Some folks are connected to flowers. Some to dirt. Some to houses. Some to the moon. Some to the Virgin Mary. I don't believe we choose who guides us. They choose.

If rose quartz is one of your guides, you could wear a rose quartz necklace or keep fresh roses, or dried rose petals, around the house. Although establishing such reminders is easy to do and a beautiful thing, it's often not enough. We usually need to *do* something to cultivate our relationships with our guides, just like with people. This is why talking to our guides is so important.

Will your friends or relatives think you've gone mad once they see your home bedecked with portraits of the great spiritual masters? Will they be confused by your altar, touching it without permission? Possibly. Use good judgement. You may want to keep your spirit guide cultivation for times when you're safely alone.

Tangent: The Value of the Unplug

Since moving back to Brooklyn, I've moved toward traditional Jewish life (again), which includes observance of the Sabbath (*Shabbat* in Hebrew). This is a period of time roughly from sundown Friday night until an hour after sundown Saturday night.

Long story short: this time is holy time (magical time if you ask me), and there are rules. There are things we are supposed to do and things we aren't. One thing we're supposed to do is eat delicious meals with others. One thing we are supposed to refrain from is work, and work in this context includes the internet.

When was the last time you spent twenty-five hours away from the internet by choice? Or even just a few hours away? Many of us check our email in the middle of the night. I'm not saying the internet is bad, but the constant flow of information and instant communication can make us lose our silence. Although our spirit guides don't mind the messy flow of our lives, silence inspires them to come closer.

Last Friday night I lit my Shabbat candles, as is the tradition. The computer had been put away, and I went to lie down. I was weary from the week. It was quiet. Immediately, I started to relax and suddenly realized not only how bone-and-soul tired I was, but how sad I felt over my cat who had died just a few months prior. Other feelings came forward too. No one ever said silence was easy, but I recommend it. And your guides will likely join you there.

In the Garden of the Guides

Your team of spirit guides can help you craft your spiritual path. How? By asking them questions: *Is this right? Am I on the right path?*

What do you think? Maybe you'll get answers in words. Maybe head nods you see in your mind's eye. Maybe feelings. Cultivate these relationships, because these relationships can grow.

Clearly that shaman had cultivated his. He knew his spirit guides well. No matter what happened during that shamanic journey, he knew who to ask for help. It's like knowing who to call if your car gets stuck in a ditch, or the subway stalls, or you're running late and the dog needs walking.

Our relationships with the Invisible World can be as real and as meaningful as our human-to-human ones. I want you to know that you have company here. You aren't ever alone.

NEXT STOP

¶ FELL IN LOVE WITH A SAINT.

FALLING IN LOVE
WITH SANTA MUERTE

I'm telling you this story because saints and other holy "people" also belong to the Invisible World, and you may find yourself drawn to them and you don't know why. It's not a straightforward story because life isn't straightforward. It happens in circles and cycles and, sometimes, confusions.

You may find yourself passionately, inexplicably attracted to Indian goddesses. Or Yoruban deities. Or Catholic saints. Or Celtic gods. You may not know what to do about it, if anything.

Who are we to say that we can only have or love what we were born into? Maybe that's not what the gods want for us at all. Is one spiritual path enough? Should we limit ourselves?

Listen, you can't help whom you love. You can't help who reaches out to you from your computer screen, or the pages of a book, or from your very soul as you're walking down a city street. You can only decide what to do next, with respect, and to follow your heart.

I don't doubt there are stories upon stories like the one I'm about to tell you here, the essence of which is that perhaps you, too, grew up one way and found yourself bewitched by another.

For example, maybe you were raised in a particular religion or no religion at all, and at some point during your long life on this earth you realized you are longing for all things Quaker, or Shinto, or Wiccan, or Muslim, or anything but what you are. You didn't choose those feelings. You didn't choose this love. It happened on its own.

Recently, I was a guest on a podcast, talking about a dear friend of mine who isn't Jewish, but felt an inexplicable desire to keep kosher. What then? What does one *do* with that?

I'm not sure what the answer is, except to tell you that there's absolutely nothing wrong with how you feel.

A Story of Mystical Longing

I'm Jewish by blood and upbringing. I even attended Jewish school for most of my life (until college). There is no explanation for why I'd wind up enthralled by Christian mysticism since my high school days or possibly even earlier. It's a mystery to me.

As I was writing this section, a memory surfaced. When I was a kid, my best friend, who lived across the street, was Catholic. We shared each other's holy days. We were children. It was pure. And I remember one Christmas Eve, looking up at the sky with her, waiting for a glimpse of Saint Nicholas, just as she would join me and my father on Saturday nights to check for three stars in the sky, which signified the Sabbath had ended.

And it must have been late high school or early college when I started building a small collection of rosaries, much to my mother's surprise. I didn't know what it meant to pray the rosary. I just knew I wanted one, or two, or three.

The one clear thing: I was having mystical feelings that were bigger than any rules or tradition I'd been brought up with. Can you relate? Did you ever want something that wasn't "yours"? It wasn't envy. It was kinship.

Rootless Wandering

Flash forward: I took a Christian mysticism class in college (barely getting a C). I saw the class listed in the course catalog, thinking, *This is the one for me*, but I barely understood what they were talking about the entire semester. Plato? Plotinus? Origen? Who? Although

I do remember one student, a boy with red hair, asking our professor this question: what's an angel? That I understood.

These spiritual feelings and longings didn't take me anywhere. One class. A collection of rosaries. A few icons of Mary. The feelings didn't increase or decrease. They didn't dictate my behavior or choices, and I wandered rootlessly like many do in their twenties.

Flash forward again, decades later, to just a few years ago. I'm an astrologer and tarot reader, doing the work I do now, having an intense year of spiritual exploration. Somehow I stumble upon a video of Mexican folk saint Santa Muerte, and I fall in love. The word *love* isn't enough. I feel bonded to her instantly, passionately. I know nothing about her, so I start to learn. I buy a book (the one I recommend at the end of this section). I search for more videos, more experts. My heart swoons when I see pictures and statues and candles, and it's nothing I can control. Jewish girl meets outlaw saint. Nothing like this had ever happened to me before.

As I said at the start of this chapter, life isn't straightforward, and the spiritual quest may be the most labyrinthian of all.

𝕱ire 𝕳eart

Some of us long so intensely for a god or goddess, or a spiritual truth, and we don't understand how it can all work out, how the disparate pieces of our lives can fit together. We have no clue how to integrate them. Who do we talk to? There's no eclectic spirituality hotline. We struggle to overcome cultural taboos even just to explore.

I remember talking to a good friend of mine when I was almost converting to Catholicism (true story). I felt so embarrassed about being swept away by these longings, which didn't feel like a choice (although I could have explained some of it astrologically). To even explore it felt prohibitive to me.

In today's world (it's 2019 as I write this), there is much talk about cultural appropriation or spiritual tourism, and when Santa Muerte came at me from the blue light of my MacBook Air, I wasn't looking to take anything from anyone. I didn't suddenly become an expert on her or Mexican culture or Aztec history. All it meant was that my heart was on fire.

ℓife ℐs with People

You can't decide whom you fall in love with, but you *can* decide what to do with it. You decide what comes next.

I want to encourage you not to push away your spiritual desire, no matter how you were raised or who would or wouldn't approve. Please don't feel guilty (easier said than done). You might convert or almost convert to another religion like I did. You may just be curious and explore a little.

Also, these interesting, confusing, out-of-nowhere attractions, or callings, give clues to past lives or even future lives. Of this I'm certain.

So if someone from another world, the Invisible World, reaches out to you, what should you do? Listen. Listen. Listen. But not just that. My feelings for Santa Muerte were not a presumption that I knew the right way to honor her. Those things I would need to *learn* from devotees. I would need to immerse myself in community and be humble.

Here's an analogy. Let's say you felt drawn to Jewish mysticism, Kabbalah. Maybe you saw a video on the internet and what you heard excited you, but you didn't know any Jewish people or the Hebrew language or anything about Jewish life. I might say: learn basic Hebrew so you

can pronounce the words correctly, besides studying what they mean. This is especially important for Kabbalah, which emphasizes the mystical power of the Hebrew alphabet. I might say: find a welcoming synagogue or community center because there will be classes. And I'd say: find people to talk to about Kabbalah, the people who, centuries ago, birthed this wisdom. Yes, it will take some effort. It's not as easy as falling in love with a saint—but if a religion or path or practice has people *alive* today for you to talk to, by all means learn from them.

When I was living in Florida, there was no Santa Muerte temple that I knew of. I was on my own. Back in New York, though, such places exist. Anything is possible.

How to Talk to the Dead.

How to Talk to the Dead

In the Jewish tradition, the land of the dead has a name. In Hebrew, we call it *Olam Habah*, the World to Come. We contrast the World to Come with this world, *Olam Hazeh*, where we are now, the world of the living, with its aches and pains and bills to pay.

Please know I am simplifying here and the ancient rabbis probably didn't call it "the land of the dead," but I do—because in this tradition, it's where we may find ourselves once we leave our physical form.

I've never seen a super-detailed description of the World to Come, what it looks like or smells like or what goes on there exactly, but I feel it as a kind of vague heaven, vast and peaceful, like an office building at midnight, long after everyone's gone home, even the mice.

The Veil Thins

When it's October and getting dark early and Halloween isn't far behind, there's a phrase I often see on social media that reminds me of this *Olam Habah, Olam Hazeh* business, that there exists *a veil* between these two worlds, the living and the dead. In late October, they say, this veil will begin to thin, perhaps into nonexistence, nothingness. This process thus allows for easier, or easy, contact with the dead, should one desire such a conversation.

It makes sense. There has to be a checkpoint, right? That on the way from the living to the dead, or vice versa, there is someplace to pass through or sit down at and take a number, like the crowded bakeries of my childhood.

I had questions though. Was it really a veil? Maybe it's a wall. Or to go with my metaphor above, a place to sit and wait. Maybe all three, depending on whom you are seeking there.

The veil, the wall, is a metaphor, of course, and metaphors barely scratch the surface of the truth in all its glory—but they help us describe how to breach the distance and longing that happens when we are separated by death from the ones we love. Lucky for us, though, there are *ways*.

Dead-Curious

So you're interested in talking to the dead. Maybe. Maybe you feel closer to them than us here with blood and bones and/or you enjoy the company of graveyards. You may have been talking to dead people since before you knew what death was or you feel a kinship with "the other side" that you can't quite explain. You feel getting closer to the spirit world will give you strength and comfort or that you'll even heal rifts with problematic dead relatives. Maybe you don't know why, but when you read this chapter you feel *yes*!

Now, you don't *need* to talk to dead people, or dead pets, *ever* at any time. It's not required for your personal spiritual adventure in this lifetime. I know professional psychics who have zero desire to chat with the dead. It's just not their thing—but if you are drawn to this practice, I have a few pointers:

You don't need any particular background to begin talking to the dead or to begin hearing from them. You don't need to have had any spooky childhood experiences. You can start any time. They're always there.

Once you begin, trust that whatever you see, hear, feel, receive is real and not something you're making up. This is easier said than done and takes practice and time. That you begin to trust yourself. (I talk about trust throughout this book—trusting your gut, your instincts, your feelings.)

Information can come to you from any or all of your senses. You may feel suddenly warm or get chills. You may see pictures or visions. You may *hear* thoughts or get confusing clouds of words. I often get thoughts or words or images that have to be translated before saying them out loud. I've also learned that chills, for me, mean that whatever I'm perceiving is *true*.

Try not to worry whether the information you are receiving is right or wrong. This, too, is easier said than done. You likely won't feel confident until someone else says to you, "Yes, you have just described the appearance (or personality, attitude, style, feelings, etc.) of my beloved so-and-so." It could even be just one detail, but a detail so relevant and heartbreaking that you know you're on the right track.

We have so many more relatives and ancestors than we've met or ever will meet. You may be tuning in to someone you don't even know exists. Make room for them.

Approach the dead with respect and reverence. Even if they are happy to hear from you or are already hanging around you, you are still a tourist in their land.

••• HOMEWORK •••

HOW TO TALK TO THE DEAD

Pick a day and quiet time when you (alone or with a friend) will be able to talk undisturbed. Set aside at least twenty to twenty-five minutes. Sit comfortably. Don't lie down. Mediumship is not sleep.

Take the first couple of minutes to get settled. You're about to do something a little different than the usual. Breathe in and breathe out a few times to let out tension.

You will use the last few minutes of the time for saying farewell, saying thank you, and bringing yourself back to the present moment. More deep breaths.

You can be creative with the opening and closing, or keep it spare. See how you feel. You may want to sing or hum or pray.

Things to consider: lighting, music, candles, incense, anything you want to hold or keep with you. All this is optional, but give it some thought. You may also want to establish an altar (see the chapter on altars in the "Real-Life Magic" section of the book).

I recommend having someone specific in mind that you want to talk to or hear from: a relative you knew, a beloved pet, an ancestor you're curious about. There's no guarantee that specific spirit will show up or respond, but start there.

Record the session or take notes after. Take notes during if it isn't too distracting. Have a pen and paper nearby.

If you're working with a partner, decide ahead of time how you will share the information you're receiving. You may want to talk uninterrupted and then signal to them when it's okay for them to talk. If you're alone, you may want to speak out loud or take notes or just wait until you're done to capture what happened.

Longer sessions are not always better, but take your time. No rush.

For the session itself: keep eyes open or closed. Your choice. Out loud or in your mind, ask the dead (person or pet) if there is something they want to show you or something they want to tell you. You can ask this repeatedly, but calmly. You can shorten it: tell me, show me, tell me, show me. Speak slowly. Then go quiet. Then ask again. Then go quiet. Do this for fifteen minutes (not including the five minutes at the beginning and five minutes at the end). Then you wait.

Messages from the dead are likely to start coming in fairly soon after you begin this process. Remember to leave space as you do this. You may even want to count to ten. For example, after you say, "Show me," count to ten out loud in barely a whisper. Then say, "Tell me" and count to ten again. Then wait ten more seconds. What do you see?

DO YOU BELIEVE IN PAST LIVES?

You Only Live Twice? Exploring Past Lives

I'm not at the Magic Cafe this time. I'm at home, my other favorite place. It's early November, and we've already had freezing temperatures in New York, but no snow. It's Scorpio season in the big city, and I know I've lived in New York before. *In a past life*, I mean. Maybe I lived in a Lower East Side tenement or a winding street in Chinatown or maybe, just maybe, Brooklyn.

Believing that you have lived before, or will live again, is not essential for a spiritual path, but exploration of past lives or even just daydreaming about them can help you start to make sense of why you're here (which is one of my favorite questions and maybe one of yours too).

Soul History

Let me back up a little: what are past lives anyway? They are exactly what the phrase says. The notion (or fact) that you have lived before, that you had other lifetimes before this one. You may have been another gender or sex or ethnicity or class. You may have had many previous lifetimes or just a few, living centuries ago or more recently. Some folks (and I know this from personal experience) have had so many lifetimes that it can look like unbroken links on a chain in the mind's eye. Here's another truth: you may dig into past lives, yours or others, and not recognize yourself at all. Think about that the next time you look in the mirror, that your past goes way, way back, deeper and wider than we normally imagine.

TRUE STORIES & TRUE BELIEVERS

When I talk to friends or students or clients about past lives, I know I'm on to something when they freak out! In other words, when what I'm telling them elicits a strong reaction. They get emotional. And it may not be one of the "good" emotions. Recently, I was talking to a friend about her past life as a wealthy woman in the 1700s. I saw her clear as day wearing those ornate dresses, and with powdered hair. My friend practically growled at me, "I hate those dresses!" She's an independent woman with a big career, and what she saw as the powerlessness of the women of those times really bothered her, especially the restrictive clothing of that era. Even though we don't always recognize who we've been and where we've been, when a past-life conversation brings up super-strong feelings, it's a sign. Pay attention to that sign.

Another scenario is when two different intuitive or psychic readers of any kind, years apart, tell you the same thing, whether it's past lives or spirit guides or something else. This happened to me! I had two different people see the same "spirit guide" around me. This guide had so many specific features and both people described him! It was clearly the same "person" they were seeing. It was too uncanny not to be true. Now, this isn't to say that a one-shot vision or only one person seeing a spirit guide or past life makes it less true—just that multiple witnesses makes it easier to believe. I became a true believer in that moment.

Are There Special Techniques for Past-Life Expeditions?

I want to be honest with you. For me, there aren't that many distinct ways of tuning in and trying to get information, stories, guidance from these Invisible Worlds, whether I'm seeking the recently dead or long-ago ancestors or angels or past lives. I use the same basic structure. Maybe I'm boring. I decide who I'm looking for, and then I get quiet. It's like letting down a curtain. I don't wear a red shirt for past lives and a green one for spirit guides, but you can do that kind of thing if you want. It's one big sea we're fishing in and hopefully we catch something. Setting an intention for who or what we're trying to reach can be helpful, but no guarantee.

Let's say you want to explore your Aunt Jane's past lives. And let's say you declare this intention to the universe out loud and you light a candle and you turn off the overhead light to set the mood and you get quiet and you breathe in and out and your Aunt Jane is sitting there waiting for some past-life fireworks, the movie of her lives.

Well, sometimes the lines get crossed. Sometimes the movie doesn't start. It's not a perfect art. You may instead channel Aunt Jane's raccoon spirit guide. Was her most important past life thus in an urban area with a growing, untenable raccoon population? Maybe. Maybe this raccoon guide is the mediator. Maybe he's going to show you a thing or two. My advice is to keep going and follow the story line. Trust that you are being led where you need to go.

Sometimes you'll get little hits, little flashes of insight, and it can seem like it doesn't add up to much, but it may, in the future. Other times, an entire past-life world will burst open before your eyes, a flood of imagery and words. Again, no room for perfectionism here. Just practice. Just openness. Just willingness to see what might be hiding under the waves. Once you get used to swimming and not knowing what you'll find, it gets easier and you're able to relax.

The longer you do this? The stronger your ability and the easier it is to get what you came for.

••• 𝕳OMEWORK •••

THREE REMINDERS FOR TUNING IN

First, try to get quiet inside. Just a little. It's a subtle action. Now, this doesn't mean you can't get past-life info on a crowded street, on the bus, or in the supermarket. By "quiet" I mean the ability to make your mind go briefly blank so you can tune in and latch on, which means blank plus being ready to catch something. Imagine psychic information like a ball heading into your hands. You can also visualize yourself pulling back a curtain, or a curtain dropping, or a door opening. You can focus on one of the chakras (something I used to do), whichever one is your favorite. That chakra is like a searchlight, busily finding what you want to know.

Second: do you trust yourself? I don't mean trusting your psychic impressions, but in your daily life. The more you trust yourself with the normal things of life, day in and day out, trusting your decisions, trusting your life, the easier it will be to trust that your intuitive hits and past-life discoveries are true and not just flights of fancy or something you "made up." The Invisible World is real, but if you have trouble trusting your own "normal" perceptions, you may have trouble trusting your third-eye visions.

Third: you absolutely can use tarot cards or astrology or crystals or the sound of the wind when you engage in any Invisible World process, including past-life stuff. The material world is here to help us bridge the gap.

ONE SPECIAL CLUE

Earlier in this chapter, I was saying that I often use similar techniques, whether I'm trying to explore a past life or visit with an ancestor or other spirit guide. There's always a kind of mediative state involved and a general idea of who and what I'm looking for.

But here is something we haven't mentioned yet: is there a country or city you've always wanted to visit and don't know why? You feel some irrepressible, mysterious longing for that land? And always have? For the music of that land? Or the food? The people? The history? Often your family is not from that faraway place, nor any of your DNA. This is a past-life clue. Don't ignore it. Explore these cultures and lands and places and cities and roads. When you get quiet and let your mind go blank and you tune in and get ready to catch an impression like a ball flying through the air toward home plate, picture yourself in these places. See where they take you.

INVISIBLE WORLD TAROT.

A Tarot Spread for the Dead (and Other Gifts)

It's winter now in the big city, getting dark around four in the afternoon, give or take a minute. If you don't like the dark, you may not like this change. The sun goes down and night comes on too soon, it seems. Our sight dims. Some of us head home right away, cook warm food, kiss our loved ones, and crawl into bed. The day is done. Now let us rest.

Some of us, however, want to haunt the night—or, at the very least, the early evening. And what better fun than metaphysical? Here is one idea for what to do with the longer, darker hours: a few tarot spreads to help you get to know the Invisible World around you.

Now, you can take your tarot deck and any of these tarot spreads to a local cafe or coffee shop or bar or other hidden place as I like to do, or you can do them at home, with family gathered round the fire. Or alone, all alone.

Just know that if you do them in the outside world, strangers may make their presence known, shyly fascinated by these mysterious cards, some afraid to approach you, while others will be bold and ask in hushed excited tones, "Are those … tarot cards?" The ones who already know what you're up to will look on knowingly, nodding their heads or hiding their expressions as you turn over cards that, at first glance, appear more nefarious or complicated than calming.

What to tell the small crowd that's now clustered around you? Simply say, "I'm looking at the Invisible World." Ask them to join you if you, and they, wish. Ask them to gaze at the cards, to walk into their stories. Spontaneous tarot on the road is one my favorite kinds.

Why Tarot for the Invisible?

C'mon, you know me already. There is no topic that we can't bring to the cards, but why tarot spreads for the dead and other invisible beings?

The cards will help you discover who is around you. You may have an inkling already or had psychic readings once, twice, three times about your spirit guides or ancestors. Maybe you're just curious what or who will turn up in the tarot. Curiosity is fine, but these spreads will do more than entertain you. Although seemingly simple on the surface, they will literally bring you to the Invisible World. The cards act as a bridge.

Keep in mind that the following tarot spreads are more for exploration and going deep than unchangeable outcomes. You and the denizens of the Invisible World are in a relationship and these relationships won't end unless you want them to. In other words, if you do these spreads more than once, the answers may change just as relationships change.

You can do these tarot spreads at any time, day or night. You can lay out the cards in any shape you like. You can do them more than once or never at all. Experiment. Do my suggested spreads, create your own, or take a pinch of yours and a pinch of mine together. Experiment. The most important thing is to take your time and to make time for this. Experiment!

Think of these spreads as gifts for your invisible friends behind the veil. They are waiting for you.

INVISIBLE WORLD TAROT

Try these tarot spreads for Invisible World connection.

Knock, Knock. Who's There?

This spread is for when you want to make contact with one specific spirit guide. Will only one guide show up in your tarot spread? Maybe. Maybe not. Try it and see.

Card 1: Show me the most important spirit guide in my life at this time.

Card 2: What do they want to tell me? Do they have a message for me?

Card 3: Show me something significant about this guide, something I need to know about them.

Card 4: What help or guidance do they provide in my daily life?

Card 5: How could they help me, if only I'd ask?

Card 6: Is there anything I should do for them?

Storming the Veil

This spread isn't your average mediumship or "show me my ancestors" tarot spread. This is for when you are grieving hard and want to make clear contact with someone you desperately miss, person or pet. I invented this one not long after my beloved cat Cleo died. I missed her so much and was determined to reach her. And I did. About a year later, I had a vision of her escaping back to the land of the dead after spending many months with me. I hadn't meant to keep her, but sometimes tarot is powerful magic.

Card 1: Is this the right time to reach you?

Card 2: What should I do to reach you?

Card 3: Who can help me reach you?

Card 4: How can I keep our connection alive?

Card 5: Do you have a message for me?

Past, Present, Future Lives

Card 1: Which past life has the most effect on me in this life?

Card 2: How can I learn more about this past life / what steps should I take?

Card 3: Show me something specific about who I was or what I did in that life.

Card 4: What is the purpose of *this* lifetime?

Card 5: Will I be reincarnated again?

Card 6: Tell me something about my next life.

Twenty–Five Cards or More

Any of these tarot spreads could easily contain dozens of sub-questions. You can always add in cards if you want more detail. The Past, Present, Future Lives spread could easily be twenty-five cards or more.

As always, I recommend you keep track of your findings in your tarot (or other) journal. I promise you'll be glad you did. Just last night I wanted to check some notes that I took the last time I got a reading from my favorite medium, and I knew right where they were (in my big blue journal)! I only wish my notes had been even more detailed.

Not So Solid After All

Why should the Invisible World jump into your collection of cool stuff? Because this earth, with its supposedly solid walls and doors, isn't enough. Because you know there's more to life than what you've been taught. Because you see through the limitation of flesh and the body. Because you already live a life of the spirit and it's about time you stormed veil after veil after veil.

TIME TO HEAD BACK OUT ON THE ROAD AS WE LEAVE THE INVISIBLE WORLD FOR THE WORLD OF MAGIC.

RECOMMENDATIONS:
IN MY INVISIBLE WORLD SUITCASE

My knowledge of and comfort with the Invisible World comes mostly from *life experience*, and not from books or other media. Maybe you can relate. It comes from closeness with death at a young age, as well as other trauma. *Hard times make us search.* My comfort with it also comes from growing up embedded in a religious structure that was mystical and magical. My clients and students ask me all kinds of *interesting* questions—about past lives, about talking to their beloved dead, about spirit guides. I try to find them answers. Life is a teacher.

Despite all this life experience stuff, though, I want to recommend a few books and authors:

Read **Judika Illes's** *Encyclopedia of Mystics, Saints & Sages: A Guide to Asking for Protection, Wealth, Happiness, and Everything Else!* For me, this is the ultimate guide to spirit guides (although Illes may or may not agree with that assessment). Despite the book's subtitle, you don't have to use it for asking for protection or asking anything in particular. You can just read it! It's a fat, fun, story-filled book. You may never get through the whole thing or maybe you will, if you're systematic about it. I also like this book for bibliomancy. Open to any page and that entry (I just turned to "Archangel Raphael") may have a message for you.

Read the books of **Aryeh Kaplan** (there are English translations) to get a taste of Jewish mysticism and guidance. I probably could include him on a few of these recommendation pages. *Inner Space* is my favorite, and I will likely never finish it. I get lost in its depths.

Read **Sandra Ingerman** for books on shamanism and **R. Andrew Chesnut** for Santa Muerte.

NOTES

REAL–LIFE MAGIC

Magic is power.

What Is Magic?

I'm writing to you from the gray world skies of Brooklyn. It's late afternoon, November, chilly and damp, but I'm not writing to you from my usual cafe. Instead, I'm in the cozy kitchen. There's hot water on the stove for tea for us, and I'm settled in for the night with you. I've got recipes on my mind, and you'll see why. In this chapter, we aren't on the road, but right here at home so we can cook. In this section of our book, I want to talk to you about magic.

Magic is possibly simpler than you think, easier than you think, and yet also harder than you think (but we'll get to that; this is the simple part). Or, maybe you don't think about magic at all, even though you've been doing it your whole life.

In this chapter, I'm going to give you my recipe for magic. Here are the main ingredients.

First Ingredient

Desire. Two heaping scoops or more. Adjust to taste.

Magic begins when you want something. It can be anything. But it starts with a desire. For example, you want a boyfriend or you want money for an extra-high electric bill, or protection because crime has risen on your block and you want to feel safer. You want a new job or a baby or for your lover to come back. You want a new home, to win the lottery, world peace. It can be personal or global, but it all starts with desire. Having a desire is the foundation, the raw material of magic—to want something and, usually, to want it very much.

Where desire exists, lack also exists, or at least the feeling that something (or someone) is missing. The urge to do magic then comes from the urge to change or adjust reality (or oneself) in some way. All magic starts here, and then anything goes and anything is possible.

But this is only part one of the recipe. There's no magic or meal with only one ingredient. It's more, shall we say, collaborative than that.

You're Already Doing It

So you're probably already doing magic and have been doing magic for years, but an unfocused or uncooked version. For example, you close your eyes and make a wish when you blow out the candles on your birthday cake. Maybe you make New Year's resolutions or set New Moon intentions. This is all good, fine, delicious magic, but it's magic part one. It's the desire part. It's the noticing that you want something else or something more.

Now, the more intense and focused your thoughts and desires, the more potent your magic can be—but is it enough to merely have a passionate thought? Of course not. We must add to the recipe. (Caveat: sophisticated magicians can do much with just their thoughts, but many of us need years to get to this level.)

Second Ingredient

Action! Unlimited scoops. Adjust to taste.

So you have the desire, and you know what you want. What happens next? We humans want results, especially the magic makers among us. *What to do?*

The answer is in the question. *We must do something.* We need action. That's the second ingredient. We add action to our desire. The action adds power. But how do we choose? How do we know what to do? How do we find ideas? What are our options?

This is where your occult library comes in. Hopefully you've already started building yours as I recommended in the tarot section (and those tarot books may or may not have ideas for your magic).

I Want You to Find Your Magic

First, let me summarize. Here's the recipe: desire + action = magic. Is that the whole story? Of course not, but it's the bare-bones outline of how magic works. You will fill in the blanks as you go, as you learn. This will be lifelong if magic dives into your collection of cool stuff.

••• Homework •••
ROOTS, REDISCOVERY, RESEARCH

Here are a couple of suggestions for how to figure out what to *do*, what to add to your desire. I'm suggesting these things because I want you to go deep.

First, I'd like you to rediscover, research your own religious or spiritual background, what you were raised with. Explore any of those familiar practices that interest you. I wonder if you can see them in a new way, that you can take what you already know and adapt it. Research folklore from your own traditions. Keep an open mind. There may be something there waiting for you that will appeal to you. Every tradition has its magic, which often gets written out or hidden.

Please know this is not a requirement but a gentle suggestion. I know some folks don't want to go anywhere near the traditions they were raised with, but sometimes a spark remains.

Second, research the history and folklore or magical traditions from spiritual paths that compel you, that call to you. Really follow your passions here. Don't let it be random. For example, you may be Jewish but anytime you read about Wicca you shake all over and want to join a Wiccan coven. You can't help it. You can't explain it. It just *is* and off you go to explore.

Love Action: Here Come the Pink Candles

Let's say you don't consider yourself Wiccan, per se, but you have a bunch of books on your shelf about spells and magic and Wicca. Maybe you've never even read them but you want love in your life and you're thinking, *Hmm maybe there's a love spell for me in one of those books!*

One of those books might introduce you to the topic of candle magic. Soon you're at the metaphysical store buying pink candles for love and red candles for passion, and even learning what the wax means when it drips a certain way or what the smoke means when it blows to the right. You might decide that on the next New Moon you're going to sit nicely and calmly for a few minutes and focus on that beautiful candle because it helps you concentrate on your desire for bringing new love into your life, and that night you start to feel how you feel when you're in love, how mushy and squishy and full of nectar and…

What I'm describing above? That's what I mean by action and adding action to desire. You did some research. You got the candles. You made a plan. You sat down, and you felt stuff. You did more than just hope. You did more than have a passing thought. You did magic.

This is one form of magic, bare bones, stripped down. There are many more.

Life Is Hard, Let's Do Spells

Why explore magic at all? Why might magic find its way into your collection of cool stuff? Because we want things to change. Because life is hard sometimes. Because it feels good to focus intently on what you want. Because magic can make us feel like we have a say in our lives, that we're not just tossed around by an angry, chaotic, uncaring universe. Within magic, we can find our power. I realize this may sound too good to be true, but how will you know if you don't try? So try.

NEXT STOP

ARE YOU A WITCH? COME WITH ME
TO THE KITCHEN AND FIND OUT.

THE WORD WITCH:
A GENTLE MANIFESTO

We're back in the kitchen now for another ingredient, a familiar one around here: a story. Gather around the table, dear star lovers. This story is about Witches.

In the previous section, I was talking about falling in love with Mexican folk saint Santa Muerte and how we can't choose whom we love. It was during that time when I started to identify as a Witch. Planet Jupiter was visiting the Twelfth House of my personal birth chart, which basically means a desire for spiritual expansion.

I was in an unhappy relationship in those days and was exploring and going deep into my spiritual life, in part to find my own power. It wasn't just that though. It felt like a storm of desire in me to *learn*.

Over about a year and a half, I began to realize that this word was already how I felt and already what I did. I had never had a word for it before and then I found it. *Witch*. I wasn't going to let it go.

ARE YOU A WITCH TOO?

I made a list for you. What a Witch is. What a Witch isn't. This is only a partial list. A Witch is someone who ... well, it depends on whom you ask.

Here is my definition. A Witch is a mindset, but also a *do*-set. Things you think and things you *do*, and of course there will be a huge range here because there are as many humans as there are stars in the sky. We won't all be the same Witch, but *we're all concerned with our spiritual lives*. I can say that with confidence. But there's something even more specific to the Witch, which I'll describe below:

Witches are concerned with their personal power, and Witches do magic. Is this true for all Witches at all times? No. But, it's true often enough.

Witches may use their personal power (which they are often found harnessing and developing) to affect other individuals (to help them *or* hurt them. Yes, it's true. Let's not pretend otherwise.) and affect the world. Or both!

Although some claim to be hereditary Witches, and these things sometimes run in families, no one need bestow this word upon you. You can choose it. You can take it. You don't have to inherit it. You can self-identify. I did. Also, we don't always know everything about our relatives. Magic, often forbidden, can be hard to trace, especially in more traditional religions.

The word *Witch* doesn't belong to Wiccans or any other religion or spiritual path. You can claim it without claiming a religion. You can be a Catholic Witch. You can be a Jewish Witch. You can add any word you want to the word *Witch*. There are Kitchen Witches and Hedge Witches and Natural Witches and Ceremonial Witches and Traditional Witches, and more. As I mentioned before, there are as many humans as there are stars in the sky, and the same can be said for Witches. We are many. We are legion.

A Witch is not a political position. You don't have to be a Democrat or Republican or Independent or Progressive or any other political label to identify as a Witch. You also need *not* be an activist Witch or fight for or against any cause or government. If you want to, that's fine, but it's not required.

To call yourself a Witch, you do not have to be psychic or a medium. You don't have to study astrology or tarot or crystals or past lives or any of the things I talk about in this book. Metaphysical studies are not required, but they often are tended to because how else will we learn about raising our personal power? There is usually a book or two in the home of a Witch.

To call yourself a Witch, you need not follow the equinoxes or seasons or understand the elements or new moons and full moons and eclipses or find solace in nature or even have companion animals. Many Witches do, but it doesn't have to be you. You can be a city Witch of the streets and the subways.

You don't have to join a coven or start a coven. You can be a solitary Witch who does their magic alone!

A Witch is not required to look a certain way. Black clothing is not required. Makeup is not required. Sexiness is not required. Black cats and broomsticks: not required. No particular look is required. Witch-ness is not about appearances. It's a soul state.

As a Witch, you do not have to study the history of the Salem Witch Trials, or

any other Witch history. It's up to you. It won't make you a better Witch, although it may make you a more educated human.

As a Witch, you can be any ethnicity, ability, race, class, nationality, sex, sexuality, gender identity, size, and shape.

Not all Witches read tarot for a living. You can have any job. You can have a totally "normal" life and do your magic.

No one has to know you're a Witch. Share it if you wish, or keep all the magic for yourself. No need for a social media campaign to announce who and what you are, but know that you'll find many like-minded souls if you do, including myself! Stop by and say hello.

••• HOMEWORK •••

AM I A WITCH? TAROT SPREAD

Pull one tarot card for each of these questions:

Am I a Witch?

What kind of Witch am I?

Now, don't go crazy adding in extra cards. Stick to just two. If you aren't sure what your cards are telling you, search online or read up. Keep reading until exhaustion hits you or you feel satisfied, whichever comes first.

WE'RE STILL AT HOME
IN THE NEXT CHAPTER.
I'LL BRING YOU RECIPES
FOR THE ALTAR.

RECIPE FOR AN ALTAR

I moved back to New York City not knowing what I would find. I'd lived here before, for over a decade, but what had changed? There was no way to know until I got there. Same neighborhood, but new apartment. Old friends, new friends, old life, new life. New York City in all its tough-love, skyscraper magic would be home again.

Moving, even when it's the right decision, is often a tumultuous adventure, an upheaval of not just the body, the person, from location to location. We aren't just packing up our possessions, some marked *fragile* and some marked *sturdy* for the journey, but transplanting our very souls. It doesn't always feel good.

Now, I'm not a gardener, but I've seen plants outgrow their pots. Sometimes moving them is necessary. I've seen them stretch their leaves far beyond their terra-cotta houses. There surely must be an adjustment period before a plant feels at home again, safe, protected. The truth is, some of us never do, but wander from place to place, with our broken roots and stems.

One way to make yourself feel more at home in the world, whether you've recently moved or not, is to make for yourself an altar.

If You Are Wondering What an Altar Is

An altar usually begins with a flat surface of some kind. Flat because you will be putting things on it, and you don't want them to fall off. You want it to be steady and solid (just like you want to feel steady and solid). The altar space may take up the entire flat surface or just a part of it. Think end table or top of a bookshelf or kitchen table or desk or a piece of furniture chosen just for this purpose. What is the purpose? The altar is the designated place or space in your home where magic not only happens but tends to collect like rainwater in a silver pail (I'll explain more about this in a second). This isn't to say that magic need be restricted to the altar, but the altar is special and, well, magical.

Holy Extraordinary Furniture

An altar isn't just a thing of beauty (which you'll see right away if you look at pictures online). And an altar isn't merely that spot in your abode where you do a spell or two.

The altar, if used regularly, becomes the very center, the beating heart of your home. Your altar is alive.

Let's say you use your altar a lot and let's say you do a lot of intense focused magic there. That altar will start to breathe. The altar will start to speak. The altar will start to vibrate, and you will feel it. Others will likely feel it, too, even if they don't know what it is. It reminds me of how I feel when I enter any holy place. That place holds the energy of the accumulated thoughts and feelings of the devoted.

Do you have a favorite room or favorite piece of furniture? Is there a part of your house or apartment that you prefer, that you like to spend time in the most? For some reason it's just where you want to be.

Any place where you spend a significant amount of time will absorb or collect your energy like that pail collecting rainwater that I mentioned earlier in this chapter. That room or piece of furniture will become saturated with you. Similarly, your altar becomes soaked with what you do there, your magic.

Your altar also becomes the home base for your spirit guides and any other spirit life in your home, similar to how your favorite room is for you. The magic you do is what calls to them, and they come running.

You Don't Have to Be Artsy-Craftsy

As with anything you want to make, you can look online and in books to see what others have done and why they did it. This is perfectly valid, and it's what those books are there for, to help you. You don't have to make it up as you go along, but it's fine if you do.

My altars have mostly been my own creations, rather than inspired by anyone else (which is probably why they're not much to look at). A beautiful altar, however, isn't synonymous with effective magic. They are two different things. You can have both or either or neither! Neither you nor your altar have to be beautiful to do magic, but if you are artistically inclined, such adornment will not only be fun but part of the magical process itself.

Each item on your altar is likely to have a specific purpose, whether practical (matches for lighting candles, for example) or beautiful (the candles themselves), and the altar can be as ornate or as plain as you wish.

The first time I lived in New York City, I had ornate, beautiful altars. These were the days of many spells for me. I would seek out the most beautiful candles in the colors that corresponded to my desires. Green is often associated with money and red for passion and white for protection (among other things). I would carefully select dried herbs and essential oils to add fragrance and texture to my altar candles, but these additions also had a deeper meaning. Each herb and oil had a symbolic thrust, such as rosemary for purification or cloves for love.

Since those years, though, my altars have gotten more spare. I stopped buying so many little things, bottles and curios, in part because I moved and then I moved again. I was always paring down. Establishing an altar isn't just glorifying a piece of furniture, but is akin to building a house, a spiritual house. These days, I let my spiritual center take root *inside* of me instead of outside. What I mean is that my altar isn't a physical thing in my home, but a place I visit when I meditate or pray, and I carry it with me everywhere. And it may change. Tomorrow I might create the most elaborate altar in all of Brooklyn with every beauty this world offers up to us, but for now I let it live inside of me. You can do this too.

You can put anything of this world, anything you want, on your altar, as long as it fits. And you want to make sure that whatever you add is compatible with your intention. For example, you wouldn't use rotten meat in love magic, and you can probably understand why.

What If I Don't Want an Altar?

Even if you identify as a Witch, any kind of Witch, you don't have to have an altar. Also, sometimes life gets in the way. You might need a moveable, portable altar because you live with other people and space and privacy are rare finds. You might have a secret altar because you need to keep your magic hidden, and what seems like a simple potted plant to your family is actually a magical herb you will use for Full Moon spell craft.

••• Homework •••

TIME FOR AN ALTAR: TAROT SPREAD

I want to get a dog. Or a cat. Or a dog and a cat. Or two cats. This is the first time in almost twenty years that I've been animal-free and I think it's time to invite a new beloved or two into my life. Now, of course, I'm not saying that having an altar in your home is *exactly* the same as adopting a pet, but I do consider an altar a commitment, a spiritual and physical one. It will need your care and time and feeding and cleaning. Here's a short tarot spread to help you decide:

Pull one tarot card for each question. Consult your tarot books if the cards confuse you.

Is this the right time for an altar?

What should my altar look like?

LET'S HEAD BACK TO THE KITCHEN NOW AND TALK SPELLS.

Anatomy of a Spell

I always have books in my kitchen, but never the usual cookbooks. Usually, they are books on tarot or astrology or magic. Maybe a book on Jewish mysticism on the kitchen table. Those are my cookbooks, instructions for how to live. I also have one big book of spells. I haven't read it yet, despite the frayed cover. I've been carrying it around with me for years.

A Spell Is Like Cooking

A spell is like a recipe to help you with your magic. It's like cooking. Often in the form of a list, a spell has ingredients (items you need) and instruction, what to do with your ingredients. Spells are also like poems, juxtaposing strange and beautiful details.

Like your altar, spells can be ornate and lush, a vineyard in full bloom, full of decorative phrases and musical cadences—or they can be simple and plain, like a wooden bench, holding you steady, rather than delighting the senses. Both are good.

A spell can also refer to those special words, again like a poem, sometimes rhyming, that announce your desire to the universe (and anyone in earshot). Some spells do obfuscate their meaning for the sake of secrecy, but at the very least the words should make sense to you. You can say or sing the words out loud or in a whisper. You can also read a spell to yourself, in silence.

We Witches believe that words have power, and that our words, combined with intention and action, can create a desired result or outcome. In other words, magic. We are announcing to the world what we want, what we intend, what will *be*. Words can help us concentrate, and the more concentrated the intention, the more potentially robust the magic.

••• 𝕳OMEWORK •••

STARLIGHT LOVE SPELL

Of course, I want you to write your own spells, so here is an example of a spell I created just for you. It's a love spell.

The purpose of this spell is to *attract* love, to call love into your life. It's a seven-night spell and candle intensive!

Ingredient List

1 cup starlight

2 cups dried rose petals

1 large rose quartz crystal (more if you have them)

28 pink candles (white tea lights are fine in a pinch, but pink is better.)

1 plate or tray, large enough and safe enough for seven candles (Seven is the most you'll have burning at one time.)

Matches and candle snuffer (if you have one)

Where to Find Your Ingredients

How to gather starlight: Sit outside on a clear beautiful night when you can see the stars. Bring with you a beloved cup or goblet or

small bowl. Collect the starlight for a minimum of twenty minutes. Imagine the stars
pouring love into your cup.

To find rose petals, crystals, and candles:
I recommend doing an online search
so that you can find special shops that
appeal to you. Spend time on this. Don't
just order a crystal online if you know that
you really need to see and touch crystals in person. There are so
many wonderful sellers and shops out there. I know you will find
places that feel right to you and that you love to visit.

Why starlight: Starlight symbolizes hope, adds an extra touch of
magic to your magic, and will remind you of the vastness of the
universe, and of your own soul. They really are the same.

Why rose: Roses symbolize love. Rose quartz is beautiful. Rose
petals are beautiful. By using more than one item symbolizing
the same thing, we intensify and magnify our intention. We are
essentially saying: *Look, I want love so bad that I won't just include
some rose petals here but a crystal too! And other stuff! Look, universe,
I'm taking the time to do this! Favor me! Grace me with a pure, abiding,
forever love!*

Why pink candles: Pink is associated with love (thus more symbolic
layering). Also, I am partial to candles in any magic or spell, and
have often wondered why this is. I don't think it's random. In my
Jewish tradition, almost all holidays, festivals, or rituals begin
(and sometimes end) with candles. Fire marks the beginning of
sacred time.

Instructions

Get your ingredients ready and then go out to collect the starlight. Do this spell right after you collect it.

You can arrange the items on your tray or plate in any formation you wish. You can put the cup of starlight in the middle and the other items surrounding. You can drop the rose petals around the perimeter of your tray or keep them in a bowl.

You will light one candle the first night of the spell and add a candle on each subsequent night so that on the second night you have two candles, on the third night three candles, etc. By the last night, you should have seven candles burning, one for each night.

Once you are ready with your starlight and other ingredients, light your candles. Close your eyes. Inhale. Exhale. Open your eyes.

Recite these words:

Starlight, star bright, bring love to me.
Starlight, star bright, I hope in thee.
Into the night, the stars align.
May true love find my love, divine.

Close your eyes. Inhale. Exhale. Open your eyes.

Sit with your candles then, just gazing, just being. Stay awhile if you can, twenty to thirty minutes, even. Then go about your evening.

NOTE: Please don't leave candles unattended. If they are not fast-burning (like some Chanukah candles, for example, which may burn as little as twenty minutes), extinguish them with a candle snuffer. If you do not have a snuffer, then blow them out. I know some Witches never ever blow out their candles, but safety matters. When I put out my candles,

I always keep in mind that this action does not extinguish the spell and that the spell is alive and well (despite practical safety measures).

During the day, cover the tray and all items with a beautiful cloth or scarf. Remove the cloth each evening once you can see three stars in the sky, and then light your new candle.

The morning after the seventh night, the spell complete, wrap your crystal in something pretty and put it away until you visit it again. It has taken part in a sacred ritual and will remember it. For items that need to be discarded, make sure to kiss them and thank them before you let them go.

NEXT STOP

TIME TO TALK ABOUT MAGIC AND POWER.

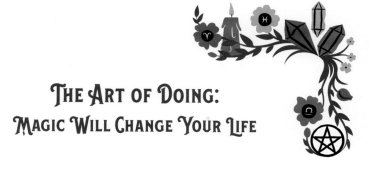

The Art of Doing:
Magic Will Change Your Life

Gather around the table again, dear friends. We finished our spell work for the night. The altar is quiet. The candles still burning are casting wistful shadows upon the wall. I've put water on the stove to boil if you'd like a hot drink in a minute. There are sweets should you want one. I want to share a few more things with you now about magic. Sit down and relax. Let's talk a little more.

Remember I said at the start of this section that magic is simpler and easier but also harder than you may think. The way that it's harder may surprise you. It's not because magic isn't real. It's not because magic isn't effective. It's not because magic belongs to everyone but you. It *does* belong to you. The challenge I speak of is magic's extraordinary ability to hold up a mirror, compelling you to face yourself. Only the intrepid Witches among us will choose to look there. Where is *there*? Read on.

You Are Trying to Change Reality

I remember the days of doing my fancy spells, buying candles and bottles and oils and magical boxes to store everything, and a couple thousand words ago I referenced a certain astrological happening and how it pushed me toward spiritual expansion and exploration. I was reading books about magic in those days, but that's not all I was doing. Reading about magic isn't *doing* magic, and there's a difference between those who talk and those who do. A theme that runs through this entire book is that *life* is found in the *doing*, the action, the practice.

And, yes, magic is a life experience like any other (sort of), but heightened, enhanced, intensified, *because we are trying to change reality*. That's the whole point. Think about that. We are trying to change what *is* into what we believe, feel, *know* should be. Sometimes it works exactly and sometimes it doesn't, but there is always a consequence (more about consequence in the last chapter of this section).

Three Things I Learned from Doing Magic

First, we aren't alone. There's more to this sometimes-dreary, boring, teakettle-commonplace reality than what we ordinarily perceive with our ordinary senses. And did you know that you can train yourself so that what seems like extraordinary, or extrasensory, becomes an everyday experience, daily life? Would you like that? Even though I've been doing psychic readings for years, making contact with a spirit or with someone's future never gets old. We aren't alone because spirit(s) are always around us, and magical *doing* helps us know this, directly.

Maybe you already suspect this is the case. Maybe you already believe in a goddess or angels or ghosts or mermaids or that your ancestors are sitting right behind you at the table. But there's nothing quite like magic to show you that you can connect, that you are the connection. You wouldn't be reading this book if you didn't already feel this at least a little.

Magic is the art of doing. Magic opens the door. And the door isn't really a door, is it? Just like the kettle on the stove isn't really a kettle. The door leads us to worlds beyond our commonplace reality and the kettle boils water for a magical elixir. I know what I'm telling you here sounds like a story or a dream, but it's a true one.

Second, magic helps you discover the terror of what you want. Yes, terror. Hear me out. If you do magic, you'll see that it works, no matter your tradition or lack of one. Put some focus on it and you'll get results, and this is what often stops people—because magic *is* effective, not because it isn't.

Many of us don't have the time or energy or *make* the time or energy to even discover *what we want* or what's there inside of us, waiting to be found out like a hungry mystery. Why would we avoid something that works? Truth: because everything would change then, the very stitching of our lives would rip. It could get scary. We'd have to face ourselves, our mistakes, our desires, fears, and years long gone.

By doing magic, you're doing self-discovery. With the trial-and-error of putting together magical rituals or writing spells, you start to see more clearly what you want, what you don't, what you've lost. It can hurt. The past pains and traumas of your life may march before your eyes.

With magic you can discover what means *so much* to you that you're willing to track down rare unusual ingredients (i.e., your dreams or goals), or bury something in the yard at midnight (i.e., your guilt, your fears), or on a full moon write a poem that rhymes (your beating heart, your vulnerability in those lines).

Maybe your magic won't work. Maybe it will. As I've said more than once in this book, you won't know until you try.

Third, do you believe that getting what you want in this lifetime is possible? Even just a little? Magic lives at this address, at the intersection of faith and belief and power. You don't have to be all-in, but you have to be willing to begin.

If you decide to do magic, get used to this idea: You are powerful. You can change your life and sometimes … you must.

NEXT STOP

HERE COMES THE LONG NIGHT.
GIVE US TAROT AND SPELLS.

TAROT & A SPELL FOR THE LONG NIGHT

Although it's not yet officially winter in the big city, we had our first snowfall last night. I watched it from one of the living room windows, snow blowing sideways through the air. I thought about going for a walk and taking pictures, but couldn't peel myself away from the scene at the window. I felt that I would see it better, understand the snow better, from a distance.

How to put magic into your daily life? Someone was asking me this question today. I told her: start looking at things, at life, at weather, at snow, differently—closer up or from a distance. Look up at the night sky, the snow blanketing the tops of the houses, and you'll see that, yes, life has always been magical. Nature didn't change. Snow has always been snow. But now you can see it through new eyes. This is one thing that the magical life, in real-life, can do for you. It can show you wonders.

In this chapter, I have something for you to do on those long, cold, wintry nights inside, or even long, hot summer days. I bring you a spell and a tarot spread.

The Tarot vs. The Spell

What's the difference between tarot and a spell? We've discussed both already, but let's review.

Think of a tarot spread as you asking questions of the universe and looking for answers, and the cards providing clues, pictures, signs, mysteries for you to interpret so that you can get closer to the truth. The act of turning over the cards is meditative in and of itself. It's a mission of seeking.

A spell, however, isn't so much a spiritual question-and-answer session (which tarot often is) but a design, an arrangement of emotion and objects and purpose.

The purpose isn't to give you an answer, but an outcome. Magic (including spells) is a more goal-oriented project than tarot ever will be, although tarot can be part of any magic or spell you do.

Also, a spell requires time (to get results), unlike the often instant gratification of a good tarot reading. This isn't to say that tarot can't be mysterious or that we get all the answers we seek ASAP, but the two are fundamentally different, and yet friends. With tarot we seek the truth or guidance or both. Magic, however, is akin to playing God. We come to create.

Of course, you can combine the two on the same evening, which is what I'm suggesting you do here.

••• Homework •••

EIGHT—DAY SPELL TO UNCOVER YOUR MAGIC

Do this spell for eight days minimum, ten days if you need more.

I recommend doing this spell when the weather is in crisis—snowing for days, a heat wave, or raining so steady it fills the pots on the stove. Do it when you feel there is nothing else you *can* do.

The goal of this spell: once it's complete (or even during!) you will begin to perceive, receive, signs and clues about what belongs in your magical life, your spiritual path, your collection of cool stuff. The goal of this spell: discover what magic is *yours*.

So here's a question: what kind of magic is there? Think of this entire book as potential magics for you to explore, learn, play with. There are others, of course, but only so much we can cover in this one volume.

Ingredients List

Tarot cards

Ten to twelve minutes each day for eight days (or ten!)

Doesn't matter what time of day

Solitude and silence for those ten minutes. Sequester yourself!

No candles or crystals or other special items are needed, but you will need paper or a journal and a pen or pencil.

Use a timer if you need. Write longer if you want, but not less. The act of writing is the magic here. The act of writing is the spell.

Here Are the Magical Questions

Write with any or all of these prompts/questions in mind. And, of course, you can make up your own. The ones below are mere suggestions.

What is magic?

What is my magic?

What magic should be mine?

What magic should I learn?

What magic do I already know?

You may get images in your mind's eye or thoughts in your head or words in your ears. You may feel led or called to astrology or tarot or spell-casting or mediumship or none of the above. You may hear whispers describing worlds unfamiliar to you in a language you've never spoken. Make sure to listen.

After you do your writing, pull a tarot card, just one. Sketch it quickly. Intuitively interpret it or look up the meaning, but don't linger, don't study it. Write down what you're thinking and feeling. Every couple days or so, review your notes and tarot thoughts.

By the end of the week, you'll have a map of your magical road ahead. Sketch that road. What does it look like? The clues and signs may make little sense at the time, but they will, oh they will.

A CAUTIONARY TALE FOR MY DEAR WITCHES AND MAGICIANS.

Magic Follows the Path of Least Resistance: A Cautionary Tale

The following is a true story of the supernatural. What actually happened that night, I can't ever be sure, but I will try to tell the story as best I can.

I'm telling you this tale because if magic is to be part of your life, there are a few important things you should know, including that sometimes the unexpected happens (no matter how good we are at magic, or life). This is often the case with any spiritual practice done deeply and/or often enough. You get more chances to succeed *and* fail. It's more than that though. Read on and I'll explain.

Return of the Shaman

Let's return to the shaman we met earlier (in "Young Shaman & Other Spirit-Guide Stories"). Remember him? He went on a shamanic journey for me and also did a tarot reading. I met him just days after the events of this story.

I can't give you all the dirty details here, but once upon a time I struggled with a difficult roommate. One might suggest that asking or telling him to leave was an obvious option, some parting of the ways, but I hesitated. Why not let him stay a bit longer and things might get better? Rents are high and who wants to live with a stranger? We had, at one point, been romantically involved. Hope felt easier than change.

Then one night I was awakened by a terrifyingly loud clang at 2:30 in the morning. I ran to his room.

What happened was this: a large, heavy, metal bed frame, which belonged to my futon and had been leaning against the wall for months, undisturbed, had fallen—onto my sleeping roommate! It barely roused him and yet could have gravely injured him, or worse. It did nothing of the sort, however, except frame him as if he were a bed, slightly smaller than the fallen frame. Shaken, I went to the kitchen window to smoke a cigarette.

DESPERATION MAGIC

Days before this incident, I had been sitting on the floor of my room, immersed in a spell. I had candles on a small tray on one of those square plastic milk crates. There may have been other items too. I don't remember now. I wasn't wishing him pain or, God forbid, dead—just gone. Out of my life. A clean break. I prayed for courage and inner peace, but my emotions during this prayer, this *spell*, were as intense as my daily unhappiness and frustration.

What the shaman said to me when I told him this harrowing tale was that magic follows the path of least resistance. Apparently, it was *easier* to get him out *this* way.

What Actually Happened That Night

Was there some mischievous entity lingering in the apartment, wanting a piece of my spell? Maybe an ancestor looking out for me, protecting me, hearing me? A golem I unwittingly breathed life into? Did I, unconsciously, move the bed frame myself, by telekinesis? Or maybe it was a middle-of-the-night earthquake in Brooklyn.

Mostly, though, I wondered how something so steady, so sturdy, could fall like that, out of the blue, and not only fall, but miss the human in its path. Someone was looking out for me. And him.

I know what you're thinking: *Dramatic story, Aliza the Witch.* Well, believe what you like, but know this: magic is wild and magic can have unintended consequences, especially when emotions are aflame. I had been sitting in front of a candle and begging, hoping that an answer would come, a solution. It was the magic of desperation, and the most desperate magic is the most powerful because the emotion behind it is so pure and strong. Frustration and intensity will pack a punch when you pack it into a spell, even if you don't mean any harm.

As I wrote above, we don't always know who is around us, who might rush in to help or push a bed frame from a wall. We can put out the call, but we don't know for sure who will answer. And not all spirits are smart. Some are foolish, impetuous, with bad judgement.

BE A WISE WITCH

Choose your spells carefully, dear reader. Think hard before you do your magic, concentrating so fiercely. Have a clear outcome in mind, defined. There is power in the words you think and in the words you say, and when combined with red-hot emotions you can create, and *destroy*, worlds. Magic is *supposed* to bring results, but when the furniture starts falling? It's time to take a step back and assess (unless, of course, falling furniture was your objective).

I don't want to alarm you, but caution you. I don't want you to take a different road, an easier one, if you feel magic is part of your spiritual city. Be a wise Witch.

GOODBYE MAGIC, GOODBYE WITCHES.
HELLO AGAIN, BIG CITY,
AND THE ROUTINES OF DAILY LIFE.

RECOMMENDATIONS:
IN MY REAL—LIFE—MAGIC SUITCASE

Evelyn Paglini is my favorite Witch. She was a frequent guest on the legendary, late-night paranormal radio show *Coast to Coast*, originally hosted by Art Bell. I love them both! She died in 2014 and Bell in 2018.

I remember the first time I heard her, probably around 2008, during a bout of insomnia and up all night listening to the radio. Years later, I found her again, a repeat of the show I'd already heard, after I'd started doing magic myself. I'm not sure how many of her interviews from *Coast to Coast* are still available online, but they are worth seeking out.

I also wholeheartedly recommend the entire **Art Bell *Coast to Coast*** archive (plus the other shows he hosted). Whatever you can find is worth hearing, no matter the subject matter, be it ghosts or aliens or anything occult, magical, mystical.

Authors & Books

I haven't read all these authors' books cover to cover, but these are writers and thinkers I trust and enjoy. To read up on Wicca, read **Jason Mankey**. For information on spells and altars, magic and folklore, read **Judika Illes** (whom I mentioned in the previous recommendation list).

Scott Cunningham's *Encyclopedia of Magical Herbs* is a good beginner herbal book for Witches (he was a prolific writer, much to choose from). I also recommend **Christopher Penczak** for books on magic and Witchcraft. He was self-publishing long before the current trend.

For Jewish magic, read **Rabbi Geoffrey W. Dennis's** *The Encyclopedia of Jewish Myth, Magic & Mysticism*, and for Christian Witches, I recommend **Thomas Keating, Richard Rohr**, and **Cynthia Bourgeault**. Keating was a Catholic monk and so is Rohr (Bourgeault an Episcopal priest). All three might find it blasphemous to be included in my real-life-magic suitcase, but I love all three, and all three influenced me spiritually. Although they are Christian, which of course is a specific belief system, their devotion to the divine is universal and so profound.

NOTES

_____

_____

_____

_____

_____

_____

_____

_____

_____

_____

_____

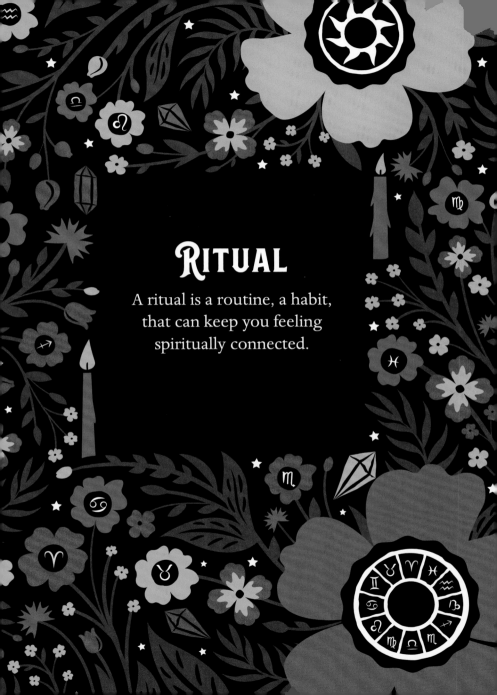

RITUAL

A ritual is a routine, a habit,
that can keep you feeling
spiritually connected.

Places & Spaces

As usual, we begin with a story.

The other night in the big city, I was out walking with a friend who plays the violin. It was dark. It was late. It was December. It was after a show. Up and down Second Avenue, we walked.

He took me to one of his favorite restaurants, where the borscht is plentiful and the ambiance dingy. They call it a restaurant, but it looked more like a hallway in someone's railroad apartment, narrow and potentially treacherous. It wasn't though. This was a restaurant of love. I could feel it.

The place was closing for the night as we walked through the door, but thank God he was able to get some of that borscht to go in a paper cup, and we walked off into the dark, down one street and then another, until the rich purple soup was gone and the stars finished twinkling in the sky.

I asked him if this was one of *his* places because I also have places, cafes and restaurants, sometimes bars, that I return to over and over. I make myself at home in them. I'm what they call *a regular*. In these places and spaces, we mingle with the workers and managers, owners, and the other patrons who have decided that this place, too, is their place.

Those restaurant folks seemed to know him well, like the ones at mine know me. And we, those of us who do this, who haunt the restaurants of the night, do so not only because of the food and the drink and the people, but because, like my friend here, we crave routine itself, the familiar. We crave ritual. We long to return.

Routine Is Spiritual and Here's Why

Doing things regularly is how you become an expert. You gain experience. We get to this land called expertise by practice or routine or ritual.

And you may say to me: *But Aliza, why do we need to become experts of cafes?*

To which I reply: It's not about cafe expertise per se, but putting routine in your life, which could begin or end with a cup of coffee in the same seat in the same place, and you notice the details of the comings and goings of the establishment, the opening and closing, and thus involve yourself in human nature and adventure. This is your spiritual life because a spiritual life, spiritual path, isn't just *special* activities like tarot or astrology or magic, but daily life. You are here. We don't walk around in the cold at midnight and not find the answers we seek. They are everywhere, but especially found while we're doing other things, routinely.

The more structures and routines, the more opportunity for inspiration. It's as though the Invisible World prefers regularity in which to insert its insights. Know what I mean? You're out there living your life, going to work, buying groceries, cleaning the house, checking the time, and the routines are all around you. You may not even notice how many of these structures you have until one day you find the answer to a problem that's been vexing you. It appeared out of nowhere.

The more you do these regular things and notice these regular things, the more you allow yourself to marry routine and the more your experiences, spiritual and otherwise, will have depth. It's like cream instead of skim milk—life becomes fattier, richer, more luxurious in the mouth.

Noticing where you have special places and spaces in your life, like a restaurant or cafe, or acquiring them if you don't already have them, is part of this process. So find yourself a coffee shop or diner or dark, quiet place just for you in the midst of the rush of the world. Sit there awhile. Go back the next day and the next.

These seemingly ordinary routines bring you to the poetry of your life. That simple coffee, that roll with butter is a portal like the beautiful tarot deck or the deepest astrology reading ever. Finding those details, observing the little things, is the beginning of understanding far deeper things, including that second cup of coffee or the movement of the stars.

WE SIT AT THE COUNTER

It wasn't only this skinny, dingy, beloved restaurant that was my friend's routine. He always sat in the same spot at the counter. I do that too. And this wasn't his only place. He had others. We had others.

My friends, the entire book is this topic: that you can (and, dare I say, should) constantly, habitually, pursue, create, seek out your spiritual path and find yourself there. Map it.

On the surface, these particular habits, such as having daily coffee at a cafe, unlike magic or mediumship, may not seem spiritual at all, and yet they are. It's the foundation of all the holy wisdom. That you get up each day and live your life.

Also, you may have noticed that I emphasize *working* with the tarot cards, for example, even more than reading books about them. How regular practice deepens your experience of what you're doing. Thus, where you go, literally, is also such a practice and a spiritual one because it opens you up so wide and so beautifully. You can bring your tarot and astrology with you, anywhere and everywhere.

A Place to Rest

Why have actual physical places on your path? Isn't all this talk about the journey and the road just a metaphor? A story? Yes and no. It's good to have a fine place to sit down and be seen, acknowledged, a place to rest your feet, a stop along the road. These places know you, they love you, they bring you what you need.

Of course you don't have to choose the things that I present to you here (cafe routines, meditation, writing), but they can help you get started. They can help you find *your* routines.

We can't just talk about it though. We have to do it, so here come the suggestions. Please proceed to the next chapter.

ARE YOU ONE OF THOSE PEOPLE
WHO SAY THEY CAN'T MEDITATE?

MEDITATION AND THE WILD MIND

Oh, this is a controversial topic. I've talked to so many sweet folks over the years who have told me they try to meditate, and they can't or they refuse it out of hand, which I understand. I don't like it either when people tell me what to do. It's like flossing teeth: good for you, they say, but tedious. What's so wrong with a little tedium though? Does everything have to be so exciting? It seems that way sometimes.

Sometimes meditation is boring, sure, but here's the revolutionary thought: it's okay to be bored.

Some complaints I get about meditation, though, aren't that it's boring, but that folks can't sit still or stop their thoughts from running around their heads (and maybe that wild mind *is* their nervous system's response to this "boredom"). I don't see any of this as a problem, though, but part of the process. Life: we don't get to have just the pieces we want, when we want, but the whole *megillah*, including the boredom or the suffering or the obsession. You get the picture.

You probably already know this. Meditation is no different. It's not heaven.

The so-called problem, as I see it, isn't with meditation practice itself but how we've thought about it or taught it over the years, that meditation is supposed to be some spotless, smooth or even "fun" experience, like a theme park, and if you don't emerge refreshed or enlightened or comatose, then it didn't happen or wasn't worth it. But it did. And it is worth it.

The key is this: the benefits of meditation, for your spiritual life in particular (because, after all, that's what we're here to talk about) happen *over time*.

I don't want you to feel guilty, though, or pressured—you don't *have* to do anything I suggest—although obviously, yes, I am pro-meditation for anyone on a spiritual road. I'll tell you why I think it matters and then you decide. The chapter after this one will have some detailed instruction.

WHAT IS MEDITATION?

For years, I did two different kinds of meditation, and of course there are many more than two. The first kind helped me feel rooted and aware, and that was its purpose. It made me  feel more *here*, conscious of my body and breath, my discomfort, as I sat for more than ten minutes at a time, in silence. I began to see how I truly felt and thought about things. This knowledge wouldn't have come to me otherwise. It helped to sit and stop.

This meditation style wasn't meant to be an escape. I wasn't trying to talk to angels or dead people or have a "spiritual experience." That kind of meditation came later for me, after I moved back to New York. It was a small class held in the evening near Penn Station. Our teacher would read to us from a different holy book each week, a page or two, as we unwound from the stressful day. He would dim the lights and turn on relaxing, wordless music. It was impossible not to zone out into the ether, and I would fall into a light trance each time. I could ask my spirit guides *anything*.

I loved both types of meditation. The first made me earthbound, present. The second made me fly.

Hear me out. Meditation isn't about killing off our wild minds. It's impossible to do so. We're alive. Our minds move. Meditation, however, *is* about slowing down and how the more you slow down, the more you see, perceive, about yourself and the world around you.

Sitting down to meditate supports this slackening. Even when the body is fidgeting and the mind is racing, the body knows something's up and it responds. It starts to calm down, cool down, away from the passions of the galloping heart and mind.

Two Reasons to Do It Right Now (Yes, Right Now)

Let's say you have no interest in getting in touch with yourself as I describe above (and surely such humans do exist). What else is meditation good for? Why bother to make time for this boring, fidgety encounter? And why put it on your spiritual map when it's easier just to keep driving?

First, along with any kind of soul-searching divination system (like tarot or astrology), meditation is the number-one method that will help increase your intuition. As I wrote earlier, I don't think I've met anyone in the metaphysical world, including Witches, were-wolves, and shape-shifters, who didn't want to get more psychic, whether for personal or professional reasons.

If you sit down every day to be with yourself, in the way that mediation allows, your intuition for sure will get more reliable and more intelligible. Like with tarot, the more you do it, the better it is, the better it gets.

Second, even if you have zero desire for knowing yourself or increasing intuition, meditation is amazing for your spiritual path because it connects you to the metaphysical realms in a big, big way. Want to understand the language of stars and ghosts and the wild lands beyond this one? Learn to meditate. That's how.

Of course, people find it frightening. They intuitively back away from meditation. Because they know. They absolutely know that getting quiet and slowing down leads to the unknown, the most terrifying land of them all.

MEDITATION IS LIKE MAGIC

One more point for now before we move on. The main results of meditation, like magic, are often seen *later*. Doing a spell is creative and beautiful and fun (just as meditation is what it is), but you are doing it for an outcome that will be *revealed*. It takes time. Maybe meditation will relax you in the moment. Maybe it won't. Maybe meditation will bring you insight in the here and now. Or not. One thing is for sure: people want their cookie ASAP, and the cookie of magic and meditation mostly happens in the future, near or far.

Meditation is so important; we can't just stop here though. In the next chapter, we'll discuss a few solutions for folks who want to meditate (and can't or won't), plus a little detailed directive.

HERE COME THE INSTRUCTIONS
FOR YOUR WILD MIND.

Making a Vessel:
Meditation for Those
Who Can't Sit Still

I'm back at the Magic Cafe, writing to you now, and remembering that story I told you about the ancient astrologer. Remember her? I've heard it upon good authority that she had intricate routines, for the morning and the evening, and these daily rituals assisted in her astrological magic. Her writings on the secrets of meditation, sadly, have been lost. Some of them she destroyed; she burned them. Lucky for us, many of her ideas were remembered and passed down by her apprentices. Some of the following counsel was inspired by her.

Ripen

Routines create space in your life and in your mind. Believe it or not, the more regular your life, the more room you have in it. Meditation is one such routine. Routines create space for epiphany—by which I mean flashes of insight, bolts from the blue, imaginative hits, psychic downloads, everything many of us spiritual seekers claim to want. Oh, if I had a dime for every seeker who wanted wisdom at the ready, a never-ending fountain, but didn't want to practice. Seekers who don't seek. But how can you get good if you don't practice? Yes, prodigies exist, but eventually we need to mature. It takes effort, though, unlike a piece of fruit sitting on a table which will darken and ripen, without any help from our magic. That's the purpose of this book—to help you ripen.

THE OLD WISDOM

I first heard the phrase *making a vessel* in a class I took years ago, a class in Jewish mysticism. I immediately started applying it to my work with astrology students in a very specific way: that astrology would be mostly irrelevant to them if they didn't have a life, i.e., a vessel. My students would cry out: *What does it mean to have a life? We're alive! Isn't that life?* They would also say: *I see you are talking about such-and-such astrological happening. What does this mean for me?*

What I discovered was that one had to have something *going on* (tending to your life purpose, on a road heading somewhere) or the stars wouldn't be able to affect you as they should (and affect you is exactly what the stars want to do). They need something to push against, to respond to, i.e., *you*. Then the stars can adequately bless you. A good astrological happening won't mean much if you don't ever leave the house, for example. Your lack of momentum, lack of life, lack of pursuing meaning and direction creates a wall rather than an opening for blessings to pour into.

Now, of course, we continue to grow old, time passes, no matter what we do, but here's a simple example: you can't win the lottery if you don't play. You have to get a ticket. So to receive spiritual wisdom and psychic hits and the deepest insight, it helps to make a space for them, to create routines for yourself, to make a vessel. Meditation is one way, a great way.

THE MEDITATION MYTHS

Common words and phrases that I hear from people about why they can't or won't meditate:

I can't sit still.

My mind won't stop.

I have no discipline.

How do I find the discipline?

Help.

None of this is a problem. I recommend that you stop berating yourself. Get disciplined with that. Then sit down, a couple minutes each day, in silence and solitude. That's your meditation right there.

Once we realize how easy it is, sometimes the walls rise even higher, but if the seeker genuinely wants to find, they will. Eventually, they realize *their way* isn't getting them anywhere, and that perhaps another way could be of help.

I'm Not Recommending You Meditate in the Bathroom, and Yet ...

These four words will help you:

Solitude: Ideally, you have a little time and space to yourself. Even if it's three minutes in a bathroom (usually the most private place in any dwelling).

Silence: Also an ideal state, and if hard to find, you can do without. I remember during a meditation class how annoyed our teacher would get with the traffic and street noise. He would get up to close the windows each time, and I would wonder why. Aren't we here to learn to deal better with the noise of life? Leave the windows open, but if they are shut, that's okay too.

Sitting: Sit on a chair or on the floor. Anywhere is fine. You can also do walking meditation around your home or apartment or out in the world—just make sure it's slower or somehow a little different than how you normally walk, staying conscious of your hips or your feet or the position of your head.

Compassion: Don't hate yourself for not meditating. Don't hate yourself because you feel you did it wrong. Don't hate yourself.

··· HOMEWORK ···

THE QUICK MEDITATION INSTRUCTION

Sit (or walk). At minimum, two to three minutes. Five minutes is better. Some meditate for fifteen or twenty minutes. Some for hours. Start with a few minutes. Increase if you want.

Your mind *will* wander. This is what minds do. It's normal. It doesn't make you a bad person or undisciplined or a bad meditator. Some minds are more noisy than others. Keep sitting.

When your mind wanders, gently coax it, return it, to some object of focus that you have designated in advance. This object of focus can be your own breath, your inhale or your exhale. This object can be a candle, and you observe the flame. It can be a spot on the wall. It can be a word or phrase that you return to. The key is to keep returning when the mind wanders. Keep bringing the mind back. Mind will daydream. It will fantasize. It will land on painful or joyful memories. Keep bringing it back, gently, sweetly.

YOU DON'T EVER, EVER, EVER HAVE TO MEDITATE, BUT IF YOU DO, REMEMBER:

Meditation is practice, not perfection.

It's cumulative: you get better at it and receive more benefit from it over time.

Insights from a meditation practice may come in the moment, but often hours, days, weeks, months later. Even years later.

Meditation, like magic, is working even when you think it's not.

One More Thing

In addition to everything I've already mentioned, the solution for people who want to meditate but can't is something I'll share with you in the last chapter of this section. It's probably the most crucial news of all, the secret of this entire book.

Why does meditation belong on your spiritual path? Because you want to *see*. Because you want to know.

Are You a Writer?
Do You Want to Write?

Writing as Spiritual Practice

When I was young, I wrote poems, and when I was young I would go for long walks. I still do. Every time I left the house, another idea would come, another word, another poem. I filled notebook after notebook with these poems. These days I still write, and I still walk, and the subway is as good a place as any for ideas to spring forth. Every New York City street is a poem and every long walk a spiritual road.

Instructions for the Poem Road

Let's jump right in with a writing-and-walking assignment here—and you don't have to write poems at all but I want to suggest *regular writing practice* as a spiritual practice, a tool that can help you figure yourself out and may belong in your collection of cool stuff. I wouldn't be surprised if this is something you already do or have done.

••• Homework •••

TRY THE FOLLOWING FOR A WEEK NO. 1 (WRITING PRACTICE)

Go for a short walk every day, fifteen minutes minimum, longer if you can.

Go for these walks without looking at your phone or talking on your phone.

Go for these walks knowing that you will pay attention to the world around you, whether it's city traffic or people or trees or birds.

Go for these walks knowing that once you get home you will write about the walk in a journal you've acquired especially for this purpose. You can also bring a little notebook and pen with you and take notes as you go.

Why Should You Write?

The answer to the question *why write?* is much the same as *why meditate?* Writing isn't just for professional writers. Putting words on paper, or fingers to keyboard, *takes you somewhere*, just like meditation, just like walking. These are practices of movement. Yes, even meditation is movement. Think about it, think about all the places you go while sitting still. The mind travels. The mind *wants* to travel. And it's all very simple, all available to you, these practices, these rituals, these routines. They are already yours.

••• Homework •••

TRY THE FOLLOWING FOR A WEEK NO. 2 (WRITING PRACTICE)

No need to leave the house this time. Make room in your schedule each morning to write at least three pages in a journal or notebook (typing is fine if you are unable to write longhand). I hear you screaming. You don't have the time. I know. Do it anyway. Wake up five minutes earlier and yell at me when the alarm goes off. Write about whatever you want: the day ahead, the food you ate yesterday, the thing your friend (or lover or sister or stranger) said that hurt you. Three pages of anything. Just write.

But why write? Writing, more than any other task, will help you uncover, discover, and process your feelings (and undiscovered and unprocessed feelings lead to all kinds of trouble, which we'll discuss in the last section of this book). For now, however, just be aware that writing is like opening a vein. You put your lifeblood on the page. Can you do that?

What Should You Write?

I recommend you make room for regular writing in your life, private writing, personal writing, no matter what form you choose: poems, stories, journal entries about your day, freewriting with no rhyme or reason, spells, recipes, prayers, letters to the dead, little scraps of paper with notes to self on the fridge. Maybe you'll seek to publish and maybe you won't. Writing for one's career isn't really what I'm talking about here, but a daily practice, the spiritual-awakening road.

••• Homework •••
TRY THE FOLLOWING FOR A MONTH (WRITING PRACTICE)

Experiment with different forms. One week, write magical spells. The week after, write mysterious poetic notes and hang them all over your home for all to see. Week three, write typical diary or journal entries of daily life, daily thoughts, observations on how you feel. For the last week of the month, do something different each day: poem, story, fragment of your autobiography. Just write.

How Is Writing a Spiritual Practice?

You may be wondering why I'm asking you to do these seemingly random bits of wild writing. Here's the reason: I want you to get into the habit of getting words down on paper each day. Not because you're a professional writer (although you may be!), but because the more often you write—a few words here, a few pages there—the more your inner voice, your inner wisdom, your inner world, will come out to play and make itself known to you, and that's *the key* to finding what you need to do, and know, spiritually. The clues will be there. But you won't be able to find these clues until you go searching, until you start writing. I promise you'll discover what you need to know and get terrifically lost in the process.

··· Homework ···

TRY THE FOLLOWING FOR AN EVENING (WRITING PRACTICE)

Time to break out the candles again. Just one is fine. A little white tea light on a pretty dish. Write by candlelight. Make an evening of it if you can. Combine it with a short meditation session. Write for twenty minutes, ideally. Write about where you've been, where you are, where you want to be—in the context of your spiritual life. Do you crave more community? To learn something new? To go deeper? Do you feel detached from your purpose? Do you know what you believe about life and death? Do you know why you're here?

NEXT STOP

DISCIPLINE IS MAGIC.

How to Improve Your Discipline & Return of the Ancient Astrologer

I'm hoping the topic of discipline won't bore or frighten you. It's something we need to talk about. It comes up a lot in conversation with my students and is one of the main complaints that I hear.

The conversations usually go something like this: *How the hell can I improve my discipline? I try and I try and I try. Nothing works. Nothing changes.* They have a goal they cannot reach and feel like a failure.

First of all, feeling like a failure is okay, although unpleasant, I know. It's a stop along the way. It's sometimes *many* stops along the way. There is no road without a failed hour, a failed year, even a failed decade.

Occasionally, I'll see evidence in someone's astrology that discipline for them is likely an impossible dream, so why bother. Truth: it can be hard for folks to acquire good habits or routines, and for some it's extraordinarily painful to do anything beyond the minimum of keeping their life together. It's like they can't help but run. It's their nature. It's built in.

Discipline: I do believe that if you have none, then none of this good stuff can happen: the meditation, the writing, the spiritual practice and ritual. A pattern *has to* arise, even an inconsistent one. Let it be consistently inconsistent, a pattern that's always aching to fall apart. We're human. We break. Trying does matter, just like that feeling of failure matters. It's all steps on the road. Process, not perfection. Remember that. You're not a lost cause.

Four Paths to Develop Your Discipline

That ancient astrologer I mentioned in "Making a Vessel" (and earlier in the book) left behind a small, philosophical yet practical pamphlet on this very topic. Here I'll be liberally paraphrasing what she wrote and adjusting her antiquated language for a more contemporary tone (including what appeared to be made-up words or words in a foreign tongue that I could not discern). Nevertheless, I've tried my best to preserve the essence of her ideas. Her pamphlet was called *Discipline is Magic*.

Path of Pleasure

The activity, no matter what it is, has to feel good to you in some way at some point while you're doing it. For example, a forty-minute meditation session doesn't have to "feel good" from beginning to end (and probably won't), but without at least a scoop of pleasure, you're less likely to find the time, energy, and discipline to try it. You'll also be less likely to return to it and try again. If along your spiritual road you are only walking down footpaths you hate, your road will become overgrown with hateful flowers.

Path of Depth

The activity, no matter what it is, has to take you somewhere. This somewhere can be horizontal or vertical but has to feel like movement, a voyage. The ancient astrologer calls this "depth." One way this depth can be expressed: the activities you are choosing need to be teaching you something. They can be teaching you about you or about the world (physical and metaphysical), but there's got to be some exciting ideas for you to bite into and assuage your spiritual hunger. That's what the astrologer means by "going somewhere," that we must go deep into spiritual practice and how we won't return to its habits unless they are juicy. She uses that word a lot, how the spiritual life and its routines need not be dry and cold but juicy and wet, like ripe fruit.

Path of Meaning

The activity, no matter what it is, must have personal meaning for you. It matters not what anyone else thinks. The meaning could be a future goal you have. For example, maybe you want to get better at reading tarot cards. The personal meaning could be that it connects you to your past, like digging into the spiritual roots and earth of your great-grandparents. The meaning could simply be that you like it or want it (whatever "it" is). If you pick something for your spiritual road because so-and-so says you should, it will eventually crumble like old cake. This is why, throughout this book, I say to you: don't take my word for it. Try these things out. Maybe they are for you and maybe they aren't. The path is a path of self-discovery.

Path of Intimacy

The activity, no matter what it is, must make you feel like you're getting closer. To what? To the truth, the spiritual truth of your life. That you feel a bond with whatever you are doing and that the bond continues to grow. Your spiritual practices should elicit feelings in you. It might even feel like kissing, or like other, more intimate practices, when you engage in your spiritual routines. And that you run to do them, and a longing is created within you for more (the ancient astrologer again uses her ripening-fruit metaphors here). Perhaps your spiritual routines bring you closer to God (or however you name your Higher Power, if you have one). Perhaps you're brought closer to yourself. Or maybe your spiritual life is ultimately about service to others. But no matter what habits or routines you choose, they must create *connection,* or your discipline, and desire, won't grow. It will die on the vine.

PRAYER AS PRACTICE, PRAYER AS MEDITATION

Recently, I've started praying every day, at least once a day. Now, in my Jewish tradition, the obligation to pray varies, depending on which authority or teacher you ask, but I have decided that at least once a day I am going to try—not only because it connects me to the divine and to my ancestors, and others, who prayed these same prayers, but I also realized (or remembered) that praying this one particular lengthy prayer coaxed me into a meditative state. It also brought me insight.

In "Meditation and the Wild Mind," I was talking about two different kinds of meditation: the kind that grounds you and the kind that doesn't, which is more floaty and trance-like and helps you access the spiritual realms. Well, this is a third kind of meditation, the kind that results from focused prayer and prayer as practice.

I didn't make a hard promise to do it every day, but it started happening anyway. Then I noticed it fulfilled all four paths that the ancient astrologer wrote about.

I started doing it a couple days a week at first, noticed the benefit, felt how it felt, and didn't want to stop. It happened naturally though. I did it because I wanted to. I continue because I want it to.

The discipline of routine isn't meant to keep us on the outside or surface of life. We're supposed to dig in. We're supposed to take bite after bite of that ripe fruit, taste its fleshy sweetness. Your spiritual path, your spiritual life should be sweet, should be juicy. Do you believe it?

LET'S HEAD BACK TO THE BIG CITY
NOW FOR A WRITING SESSION.

Writing in Restaurants:
Making Space for Epiphany

Back to the big city now to combine two of my favorite spiritual rituals: writing and restaurants. The combination of these two is one of the best routines there is, and not just for urban seekers. Your meditation practice may come in handy here, too, because getting even a little good at sitting still (see previous chapters of this section for more on mediation and how you don't really need to sit still) will help you enjoy your time that much more at your chosen restaurant or cafe. Your meditation practice, if you've been keeping up with it, will help you observe the life all around you. Your senses will open wide. You'll see what others do not see.

You may say to me: *But Aliza, I'm enjoying a delicious donut or coffee or what have you. I don't need help enjoying my time at a restaurant.* Yes and no is my answer. Sure, you can eat. I encourage it! But we're here for another reason. By doing the routine thing, the cafe jaunt, we're making space for us to have a moment, get quiet, and think about the world. We're making space for epiphany. The food is but a bonus.

The place I chose for us today isn't noisy but isn't quiet like the grave either. For once, we've strayed from my usual spot, and I picked for us a classic New York City diner, open twenty-four hours, as it should be. For the moment, it's mostly just us and a tourist or two. See that disheveled man over there? With the newspaper? I can tell he's been up all night.

There's a heavenly din: the tender clinking of silverware, spoons on saucers, coffee being poured, conversations you can overhear or tune out. And one might swear that was the subway just now, rumbling in the distance. The city waking up. If we hurry, we can grab those two seats before the snow starts to fall, as has been predicted. The morning rush begins.

For the Urban Seeker, the Restaurant Is Your Church

Why is this even magical, spiritual? My students ask me this. It's so normal, so usual.

I tell them: being in the public sphere (like a cafe or restaurant, yes) with a special assignment, with tarot cards, with a writing prompt, is one of the most magical activities there is for the spiritual seeker, urban or not. We're not in a house of worship. We're not praying. It's not a typical religious or spiritual setting. It's not even nature, another "place" where people tend to seek peace or the presence of the divine. And yet by coming in here, armed with this purpose, we change the dynamic between it, this ordinary space, and us.

Ideally, nature and churches make the soul hum. This isn't that though. It's busy and noisy. It's business. And yet right here at the diner, we are between worlds. We are the priests and priestesses of the almighty twenty-four hour restaurant, living at the intersection of daily-life din and spiritual, metaphysical throb.

That's what I tell my students when they ask why we should write in restaurants. So now, let us open up our journals or laptops and get to writing.

WRITING IN RESTAURANTS

Here's what you'll need:

Ingredient List

Something to write with: pen, pencil, etc.

Something to write in: notebook, journal, loose sheets of paper, sketch pad

Computer or tablet or phone if you want or need to type

Tarot cards

Sweater in case you get cold (says the Jewish grandmother in me)

Writing Prompts & More

The writing prompts I have for you are questions or ideas or instructions to get your introspective, contemplative feelings flowing. Why? To wake you up. To open your senses.

Setting the Scene

Sit at your restaurant or cafe for at least an hour. Make sure you have enough time so that you can gaze out the window or lose track of time, in addition to writing. You're there to sit, to let what you grasp through your senses come into focus and then out of focus, back and forth like waves. The goal is to create a sweet meditative experience for yourself while probing your inner world.

Pickles and Coleslaw Included

It's like an early-bird special. Choose one (or two) of the prompts below (there are four options), and then definitely do the final one. The first prompt is to calm you down, energize you, warm you up. It makes you go within, like the best meditation does. Then you are primed for the questions about your spiritual life.

Prompt One

Using your sense of sound, write down what you hear in the restaurant, and from the outside world seeping in. Ignore your other senses. What do the sounds remind you of? Where do they take you? Write about what sounds you wish you were hearing. It's fine if the sounds lead you to other topics, spaces, and places.

Prompt Two

In prompt two, I challenge you to write down everything you see. Ignore your other senses. Is it easy to separate them? What do you see in front of you, to the right, to the left, behind you? What's going on outside? What or who catches your eye? What do you wish you were seeing? Is there someone you wish were walking toward you or a written message you hope to receive?

Prompt Three

Are you happy right here, right now? Write about where you wish you were and why and what's going on there. Maybe your wish is fanciful (I wish I were on Mars) or practical (I wish I were at work). How different is that place from this place? Let yourself wish completely, with all your heart. Use all your senses.

Prompt Four

Pull a tarot card from your deck. Do this with or without a question. Write about what the card means to you. Describe the image in detail. Don't worry about any book meanings. Focus on how the card makes you feel. Choosing this prompt will help you get to know the cards in a deep way, born from your life as a restaurant regular and lover of spaces and places.

And Then Answer These Questions

What is my spiritual life about at this time?

Am I happy with it?

What do I want less of?

What do I want more of?

How am I doing?

What is my heart telling me?

Why Writing Is So Incredibly Good for You

Something interesting happens when you take a thought or a feeling and try to put it into words. It happens so fast too. I never stopped to analyze those microseconds between thought and putting words on paper, until this moment. What I realize, besides how fast it is, is that it's also slow. You pause. There is space. You pick up the pen again. Write. Put it down. More space. There are gaps of time. There is a gap between thought and words on the page that can feel like a stretch of sea going on for miles. And somehow you pluck those words out of the waters. It can bring you great peace, this writing practice, writing process. I hope you will give it a try.

THE MOST IMPORTANT INGREDIENT FOR DEVELOPING, CRAFTING, INVENTING, DISCOVERING YOUR SPIRITUAL PATH, YOUR SPIRITUAL LIFE, WHAT BELONGS IN YOUR COLLECTION OF COOL STUFF.

Devotion & Tarot Magic for Good Habits

Devotion is the missing link in all this talk of routine and discipline and habit and ritual, the crucial ingredient I keep warning you about.

What is devotion? Well, I have my own idea of what it means, how it feels, but when I looked it up in the dictionary, I felt its definition didn't go far enough. For our purposes here, think of devotion as the most intense love there is. The flame of devotion may sometimes flicker, but it never completely goes out. The fire stays alive.

Without devotion to our spiritual practices, we have nothing but a dry branch of a list of things to do—and yes, I know that's plenty for some of you, but not for all. Some of us need more. We need emotion. We need longing. We need love. And *then* we can do the thing. Then we can sink into the arms of habit. Then our discipline can arise.

Without devotion, there's no drive, no power, no passion. Knowing something is good for us isn't enough. Even knowing the outcome will be amazing (like improving intuition from doing tarot all the time) isn't enough. It has to go deeper. It has to penetrate. Devotion, like desire, can't be faked.

Sometimes I substitute that word *desire* or even *obsession* for the word *devotion*. Think of it as three shades of the same, or similar, color: pink, red, bloodred. With devotion, you'll *run* to do the practice. That's how you know it's for you, and the potential is high you'll stick with it. It's this combination of devotion to the thing and creating a structure for the thing that will nearly guarantee your success. One without the other will leave you hungry, empty, searching for something else to fill you.

You'll recognize devotion because you'll feel it in your body as sensation. Devotion isn't something you think or hope. It's something you *feel* (and we'll be talking more about feelings in the next section). You might feel butterflies or tingles or pulsation or heat. It's physical. You may even feel nausea.

I'm sure you felt it already as you thumbed through this book—or not. You read the astrology or magic chapters and felt yourself come alive, felt excited, or it left you cold or uncertain. Your body knows yes from no.

And you may say to me: *But Aliza, I'm out of touch with my body. I don't understand my body signals. I can't feel my devotion.* This is perfectly normal, but think of it this way: this book can help you get better in touch with your body, and thus your desire, and thus your spiritual devotion and practices. We're here together to help you figure this out.

Tarot & Magic for Better Discipline & Devotion

The following spell will help you improve your discipline, no matter the spiritual routine you want to include in your life.

••• Homework •••

ROPE SPELL

The following is what I call a rope spell. The rope is symbolic, just like rose quartz in a love spell is symbolic (of love). In this case, however, we are symbolizing, externalizing, the feeling of being bound, as this spell is to help you with your discipline, your ability to stick with something, to bind you to it, marry it. This spell is not about *other people* (binding someone to you or you to them), but is between you and you, you and your follow-through.

Let's say your intention is to become good at spell-casting and to practice once a week. Or maybe what you want is to pray every day, in the morning, without fail. This spell can help. Read the instructions all the way through before beginning.

Ingredient List

Red candle (the bigger the better as long as you can burn it safely). Red for passion.

Candleholder, if the candle is not already encased in glass.

Plate or tray that is safe for burning the candle.

A spool of black ribbon (this is your rope). Black for gravity. This spell is serious.

Scissors or small knife.

Instructions

Do this spell after the sun goes down. Assemble everything you need. Make sure your room has enough light because you'll be working with sharp tools. Find at least thirty minutes of privacy and quiet.

The spell starts once you light the candle.

Begin by lighting the candle on a fireproof plate. Then, cut and tie a piece of ribbon, your "rope," around each of your fingers. You don't want it too loose or too tight. Don't knot it. Then sit with your palms up, resting on your knees or legs. Remember, the cutting of the ribbon is part of the spell. It should be done with intention and precision. You are being bound to your spiritual desire as you wrap the ribbon around each finger.

Then, imagine/visualize the spiritual life you yearn for. See yourself in perfect peace, going about your day, with plenty of time for your spiritual routines. See yourself happy while doing them. You can even imagine this ideal spiritual life entering your body through your palms while you focus your gaze on the candlelight. It's also fine to close your eyes. Keep seeing, keep hearing, keep feeling exactly what you want in vivid detail. Do you want to be a priestess, a shaman, a sorcerer, a psychic, a Witch? Perhaps you already are. Imagine it. What do you see? How does it feel? How do you get there? Make sure to occasionally look down at your hands. That ribbon around your fingers symbolizes your marriage to the spiritual life you want, the life that can be yours.

Continue for at least twenty minutes.

NOTE: before you begin the spell, you may want to assign a particular image (or word) that signifies your ideal spiritual life. Having a ready-made image or word to latch on to can help you concentrate even if you depart from it. For example, let's say you are emotionally devoted to a particular saint but want to incorporate regular practices. You might choose a favorite image of this saint and begin the sitting period of the spell with that image in your mind. Truth is, though, the spell will likely take on a mind and spirit of its own, as meditation by candlelight often does, but this image (or word) can anchor you.

At around the twenty-five minute mark, cross one wrist over the other and squeeze both your hands tightly, making fists. Hold them like that for ten to twenty seconds, squeezing tighter and tighter as the seconds pass. Feel your passion get stronger and stronger like the candle flame as you do this. (If you are unable to do this part because of arthritis or other health condition, you may visualize it. *It will be just as effective.*) Know that this squeezing is amplifying and solidifying and consecrating your intention. You may even start to shake!

After twenty seconds is up, open your hands. Let them hang loose and limp at your sides or rest them on your legs. The spell is done.

Breathe in. Breathe out. Blow out the candle. Remove the ribbon from your fingers, and I want *you* to decide if you should save it or let it go. No matter what you choose, make one long ribbon from these ten pieces of ribbon by tying them together, end to end. Then either kiss it and dispose of it or place it on your altar. Tying the ribbon back together symbolizes your commitment will not be broken (unless you choose to break it).

Do this spell as needed, or once a month minimum, to refresh your discipline and devotion.

··· 𝕳OMEWORK ···

BIG DISCIPLINE TAROT SPREAD

This tarot spread will help you explore your discipline and your devotion. Are your rituals and routines good enough? Are they inspiring you? Pull a card for each of these prompts. Feel free to add additional cards for clarification, if desired. Lay out these cards in any shape you like.

Card 1: Show me my discipline these days (regarding ability to set spiritual goals and stick to them).

Card 2: What blocks me from good habits at this time?

Card 3: Show me my past regarding good habits and discipline.

Card 4: Show me the near future: will it get better?

Card 5: Show me my longer-term future: will things improve?

Card 6: What should I do/what do I need to increase discipline or ability to stick to my spiritual goals?

Card 7: My spiritual practices at this time look like this:

Card 8: How devoted am I to my chosen path(s)?

Card 9: Are these the right path(s) for me?

Card 10: What needs to change (if anything)?

Card 11: Next steps regarding my discipline.

Card 12: Next steps regarding my devotion.

Card 13: WILD CARD: Anything else I need to know about any of this?

Let's say you try the spell and you try the tarot spread and you discover that nothing you currently have in your life, spiritually, suits you. Your practices and your interests may be dead, part of an old life or an old you. You may need to start over completely. Your body will tell you. You can trust it.

IT'S TIME TO SAY GOODBYE
TO DISCIPLINE AND DINERS FOR NOW
AND ENTER THE LAND OF
MOON PLUTO MAGIC.

RECOMMENDATIONS:
IN MY RITUAL SUITCASE

If you're reading this book straight through, you may notice my recommendation lists get shorter, the suitcase gets smaller. What once was a check-in bag is now a carry-on! Tarot and astrology, the subjects that begin this book, are learn *and* do topics, stuff I've read a lot about and have resources to share. These later sections are less about reading and more about *living*. Books can only take you so far. Eventually you have to put the book down. You have to practice the practice. Nevertheless, we're not going on the road empty-handed.

For guidance on meditation, and life itself, read **Pema Chödrön**, American Tibetan Buddhist nun. Reading her books (and listening to her audiobooks) got me through my twenties and thirties. Her stuff also fits nicely in the Moon Pluto Magic suitcase (find out why in the next section). Read **Dainin Katagiri**, from the Zen tradition, also for meditation and daily life. My favorite book of his is a collection of his talks, called *You Have to Say Something*.

I often talk about daily life as the poetry of your life, and I recommend you read poetry, whether you're a poet or not. I'm a big fan of anthologies. When I was a teenager, I read *The Norton Anthology of Literature by Women* (it was my sister's and had tons of poetry in it), and there have no doubt been countless new editions since then. Anthologies are great because you get a sample of each poet, and then you can purchase individual volumes if you wish. During my grad-school days, I loved *Another Republic: 17 European and South American Writers* and also the poems of **Rainer Maria Rilke** (translated by Stephen Mitchell) and **Jack Gilbert** and **Jorie Graham** and **Brenda Hillman**. It's impossible to name them all, but those were some beloveds. The good thing about individual volumes of poems (if you still buy books) is that they are easy to take with you on the road in your purse or suitcase or backpack, unlike anthologies which can run big. E-books, of course, solve that problem. I recommend you have poetry with you all the time—in real books, on your phone, hanging on the wall, in your heart, everywhere, everywhere, everywhere.

NOTES

MOON PLUTO MAGIC

Moon Pluto Magic is here
to help you with your intense
and powerful emotions.

What Is Moon Pluto Magic?

A little astrology talk now as we return to where we started, the Magic Cafe, and begin our exploration of Moon Pluto Magic. I'm convinced the cafe will be around forever, that centuries from now it will still be alive at all hours, like a New York City street, even though you and I are long gone. Sit down. Let's talk.

What is Moon Pluto Magic? Strategies and spells and tarot spreads for emotional peace. It's more than that though. It's a belief that your emotions are okay, no matter how fierce, frighting, or wild they are.

"Intense Emotions," He Said

In astrology, the moon is associated with feelings, and planet Pluto with intensity or power. And I've told parts of this story before, how I was getting an astrology reading, my first from my teacher, and the first thing he said to me was what this section (and subsequently my own astrology blog) is named after: *Moon Pluto*.

"Intense emotions," he said. He pointed to this thing in my birth chart (the moon and the planet Pluto sitting next to each together, almost overlapping), which was, so I learned, in large part responsible for a lifetime of intense, powerful, sometimes painful emotions. If I had been born even a day later, I would have had a different moon and a different personality, for sure less intense. *Timing is everything.*

In that moment, my life changed. I fell in love with astrology and I felt seen. I also realized that *who I was* wasn't my fault, after decades of guilt and shame for my "oversensitivity." Instead, this Moon Pluto thing was just something in my personal natal chart. It was neutral. I was born this way. I didn't create it. It created me.

I started to understand that my job in this life was not to repress or subdue these feelings, but to let them flow and not fear them, learn how to manage them, master them, inner work I'd already been doing since my twenties. Now I had astrology on my side too. Moon Pluto Magic was born.

Consoling, Liberating, Transforming

Being alive, being human, is like a twenty-four-hour cafe. It doesn't stop. It doesn't close. There's always another waitress, another slice of pie, another hunger. Having intense emotions is similar. There's always another opportunity to feel something so deeply that the stormy moods knock you out of this world and into another galaxy. I make it sound better than how it actually feels.

Know this: you don't have to have this Moon Pluto *thing*, like I do, in your own personal natal chart to have this intensity. Your astrology may be the complete opposite of mine, and yet you identify with everything I say here. Being a highly sensitive person or having powerful feelings can show up in all kinds of ways in one's birth chart—it just happened to show up this specific way in mine. I believe it was meant to be.

No matter what's going on in your specific astrology (and you don't even need to know the details of it, although, of course, I encourage you to learn them), Moon Pluto Magic might be able to help you embrace who you are.

There Are Three Main Branches to Moon Pluto Magic (and They May Overlap)

They are:

Magical strategies that are consoling.

Magical strategies that are liberating.

Magical strategies that are transforming.

 ### BUT ALIZA, WHY WOULD MOON PLUTO MAGIC BE PART OF MY SPIRITUAL PATH OR HELP ME FIGURE OUT WHAT BELONGS THERE?

Because you're human. Because humans have feelings! Even though you're figuring out your spiritual life, which is fun and profound, life can be tumultuous and our feelings get feral sometimes. It's good to know what to do *with* them and what to do *for* them when this happens. For you, it may be a rare thing, not your usual. Moon Pluto Magic might help you a little.

For others, it hurts to be alive, and they need to let the pain out without damaging themselves or anyone or anything. Moon Pluto Magic might help them a lot.

And we need both, we need our feelings on board as we decide where we go spiritually. Remember the chapter about devotion in the previous section? Devotion (which is definitely an intense emotion) is what ultimately drives your spiritual life. Not law, not custom, not what your family wants for you, but the heart's desire, i.e., how you feel.

The other day I was talking to a student about this very topic. She was approaching her spiritual life in an intellectual, analytical way and wasn't feeling "connected to spirit," as she put it. I wanted to know what moved her, what she couldn't live without. Did she know what was in her heart? Moon Pluto Magic is heart magic.

Also, for you, it may *not* be that you have obvious, intense emotions, but that you cannot locate your emotions at all; they are buried, and your feelings are hard to access, behind a wall. Two sides, same face. The suggestions here may help you too.

Your Feelings Are Holy

Remember that the goal of magic is to transform reality, to change what currently *is* into what we believe it should be or what we prefer.

Everything in this section, then, is guidance and love for your emotions, whether that's giving them something *to do* or something to think about so that you can deal with the feelings and yourself better. Each moment demands its own response. Sometimes the guidance is to do nothing at all. As we get deeper in, you'll see what I mean.

Moon Pluto Magic isn't just practice and homework, though; there's a belief attached to all this—that your feelings are okay. Your feelings are holy, no matter how overwhelming or overpowering they feel at times. Repressing and dismissing doesn't work, but tarot and spell work and moving your body very well may.

It's About Love

Ultimately, Moon Pluto Magic is heart magic, love magic, self-acceptance magic, kindness magic. It's about giving to yourself what you likely already give to others. Room to breathe. Compassion. It's about loving the tender, raw soul inside of you and the idea that you need not abandon yourself, even though others may have when they saw you or heard you or felt you.

If you tend to your emotions, then your spiritual path will start to become more clear, more bright. This is why we're here, talking about astrology and magic and tarot and ritual and all the other good stuff—so our direction and purpose come out of hiding. And if this isn't the sacred work of our life, then I don't know what is.

In the chapters ahead, I'll share some of what has worked for me over the years.

MOON PLUTO MAGIC
TO CALM YOU DOWN.

Moon Pluto Magic
for Consoling

I'm writing to you from Capricorn Season. It was the solstice just a few days ago. Winter holidays are underway, and the New Year is in front of us. The snow on the ground sparkles like stars. I never do much on New Year's Eve, although when I was a kid I watched the ball drop in Times Square on television. This year I plan to be cozy at home with my New Year magic.

Consoling, Rooting, Settling

I mentioned in the previous chapter that there are three main branches to Moon Pluto Magic: consoling, liberating, and transforming. Or, put another way: settling, stirring, and creating. Soothing, sweating, blasting.

All Moon Pluto Magic is self-care and situation specific. What you need will depend on how you feel and what's going on. Checking in with yourself is, thus, part of the process. If you start to practice Moon Pluto Magic, you will get very good at this, good at checking in, good at naming, and good at identifying how you feel and what you need.

The consoling strategies are the ones that help you lighten, unwind, untangle your tension. They aim to relax you or distract you or comfort you. Soothe and settle. Grounding and rooting like the Pentacles suit of the tarot, the suit of earth. Solid.

These strategies aren't for *making something new* with the emotion or releasing it or trying to dramatically change it. Those approaches would be too much upheaval, too violent. Instead, here, we are simply lowing the volume.

Consoling Moon Pluto Magic may help you with:

- A hard day.
- Heartbreak (new or old).
- Churning brain.

THREE TO CONSOLE

Need to calm down your whirling, swirling brain and body? I have ideas for you.

Moon Studies

Since the origin of Moon Pluto Magic is the moon herself (representing our feelings in astrology), moon studies is first on the list. For this, you will need an astrological or Witch's calendar (see my recommendation at the end of the astrology section).

What sign is the moon in? What phase? Do you even know the phases of the moon? Sometimes I forget what they mean. Is there a New Moon or Full Moon coming? Are we close to an Eclipse? Put your attention on this moon stuff.

Let's say you had a hard day, work was stressful, and you have some time to yourself in the evening. You want to engage with your spiritual life, but in a relaxed, easy way. You aren't feeling overly ferocious, just drained, and in need of a little inspiration to shift your attention away from the difficult day.

Take out your calendar then. You see that the Moon's in Cancer. You remember that Cancers are in tune with their emotions and tend to be sensitive to others' as well as to their own psyches. You may also notice it's a Full Moon, and emotions run high on such days, so getting to sleep early could be a good thing.

The key is to not overwhelm yourself with information, but to step out of the day and look elsewhere.

Philosophical Tarot

With philosophical tarot, you aren't going to ask life's most stressful questions, which are often our immediate concerns about love or family or work or money or the future. Because we're calming down with this branch of Moon Pluto Magic, the goal is not to ask triggering queries, but fun ones or bigger, abstract, or philosophical ones.

Here are some examples: Is there life on other planets? Will there be a female president of the United States in my lifetime? What's she like? Or, you can do personal ones such as: Show me my true nature. Show me my partner's true nature. Show me an important past life. See how these are different than more specific, predictive questions?

I would definitely stay away from: Will he text? Will I get the job? Will I make more money next year? These will no doubt raise your blood pressure if the answers disappoint you. Save them for another day.

You can also offer to draw cards for others, if it relaxes you. Tarot engages the body in the most delightful ways: we're always touching, picking, shuffling, cutting cards, which can take you out of the hard day and into the tactile world of the spirit.

Sensory Spells of Peace

Because we are trying to calm you, quiet you, root you, Moon Pluto Magic spells gently engage the senses. Dim the lights for this spell. Just one candle is fine. Sprinkle a drop of your favorite fragrant oil on the candle so that when you light it the aroma will perfume the air.

No other spell craft is required here, only that you have an intention to rest. Knowing which scents you prefer (and that they prefer you) is something you may already know and you may already have them on hand for hard days and heartbreaks. This is also why it's important to begin your personal occult library, as we discussed earlier, including herbals.

Herbs and oils have spirits and minds of their own, so if you want to slow down, you aren't going to use something stimulating like ginger. You may choose rose, which is milder, but you also need to experiment because you never know what effect plants will have on you until you walk with them.

Similar to philosophical tarot, you aren't doing anything here that will be overly exciting, but a kind diversion and stoking your senses.

After you light your candle and the scent of it sweetens your room, go about your evening, doing whatever you need to do, but

keep in mind that you have lit this candle with a pure purpose. You are connected.

Why choose Moon Pluto Magic for your collection of cool stuff? Because self-care is spiritual.

Moon Pluto Magic for Liberating

Moon Pluto Magic for consoling feels like the Pentacles suit of the tarot—grounded, rooted, earthy, practical, soothing, distracting, gentle. Moon Pluto Magic for liberating, though, is like the Cups suit or the element of water. It has to flow and flow big.

The idea is to *let go*, to release through motion the emotion. It might be through tears. It might be through sweat. It might be through singing. The emotion has got to come out of the body, the psyche. We can't just distract ourselves. We can't look away. We can't just read a book. When we need to release feeling, we are past the point of mere study. Instead, we need to stir the feelings around and let them rush out in a torrent.

The F Train & the Rain

A story: I had a circuitous subway route today. It involved not just an easy transfer of trains, like walking across the platform. I had, instead, to leave the station and walk a few blocks. The problem was that I didn't know the neighborhood and didn't know where to go. Another problem was that it was pouring rain and even though I had an umbrella, in my experience, umbrellas fail.

I walked up to a woman to ask for directions. She couldn't help. I asked another and she told me in fine detail exactly what I needed. We were standing at the edge of the curb, by the crosswalk, and nearly got splashed, head to toe, when a car sped by. I cursed the rain. She looked at me aghast while smiling, telling me not to insult *her* rain because rain brings prosperity! She said it a few times. "Get wet," she exclaimed. "Get wet!" I think she was a Witch and this was one of her many magical incantations. For all I knew, I'd just encountered the most powerful Witch in all New York.

Liberating, Stirring, Sweating

The liberating, stirring, sweating techniques are for when the emotions feel hot, sharp, edgy and the urge is for overwhelming exorcism, to get the feelings out. It's like shaking up a can of soda. You open it and it sprays all over. It has to. It has to explode. The liberating, stirring, sweating techniques are like that soda can or getting splashed by the rain when a fast car drives by. At these times, the feelings need to be liquefied and poured out! The calming techniques are the opposite: no exertion required. No exertion preferred. *Liberating* is an aggressive approach, and by aggressive I don't mean lack of self-care or hurting oneself, but taking your intense emotions and rerouting them just like I had to do with the subway. Let them pour.

Liberating Moon Pluto Magic may help you with:

- Anger that feels like tears, anger mixed with tears.
- No clue how you feel, but you have to *get it out*.
- At a loss for words but you need to speak (or scream).

••• HOMEWORK •••

THREE TO LIBERATE

These three may not seem overly "witchy" or metaphysical, and yet they are. They are three of the best Moon Pluto Magic techniques, especially when your feelings frighten you.

Need to Sweat

Move your body, according to your desire and your ability. It doesn't matter what the movement is, although it is best if you get heated up and sweat. Remember, we are trying to exorcise emotional demons here. Moon Pluto Magic isn't about "fitness" or weight but pushing yourself at least a little past comfort. That's the moment when the emotions are done stirring and aching and start to fly out of you.

I remember once doing these floor exercises that were so hard, I started to cry. It wasn't dangerous, just challenging. I wasn't searching for emotional release that day, but there it was. Again, I'm not talking about self-harm or causing yourself pain (unless pain is what you seek), but there's a threshold you need to step beyond, where relief lives.

For you it might be stretching and you hold those stretches longer than usual. It might be walking, and walking longer or faster. It might be lifting heavier weight. Often the body gets coiled tight when the emotions are freaking out, so engaging the body, pressuring the body, is excellent Moon Pluto Magic.

Powerlifting was something I wanted to do for so long, and with one lift I was able to release so much emotional pain, which then led to emotional clarity *and* spiritual clarity in the weeks that followed.

I keep telling you that this connection exists, the connection between the emotions and the spirit, the spiritual life, but you can't just take my word for it. You have to see for yourself.

Need to Cry

I have this fun, masochistic habit of listening to the same song over and over, for hours. I can do this with a favorite movie too. I keep returning. Why? It soothes me, it's calming, hypnotic, inspiring. I slip into another world. It's escapist. I slip into *that* world, the world of the song or the show. I forget my own life. Well, you know what I'm going to say, right? Moon Pluto Magic for liberating isn't to mellow out or tranquilize. That would be too cuddly. What's required is *the cry*.

Have you ever met a person who couldn't cry or didn't want to cry? Can you imagine? All that emotion, possibly decades of it, stuck in there, rotting. Now imagine all the energy it takes to keep it underground.

With the crying method, you search and you *find* that song, that television show, that movie that will make you cry so long and hard you feel your head will explode. I know I'm being dramatic, but listen: we Moon Pluto people, we already *are* dramatic! And sometimes what's needed isn't a balm but a bomb, and, in this case, a bomb of tears.

Need to Speak

This is about having a witness, a friend. Even just one. Or maybe it's a therapist or a trusted tarot reader, but it's someone you can talk to and unburden yourself. In the Jewish holy book, the Torah, there are these pivotal moments when God speaks to man. Have you heard this voice in your own life? This urge to speak, the *need* to speak, is so powerful that even the creator of *everything* (according to the Jewish worldview) stoops to speak to his creation, this little human.

Like the divine, we also must speak, and this is the third liberation strategy here. We had the body, we had the tears, and now the words, the expression, the *self*-expression, must come. How you feel, what you think, in words. Being heard. Having a witness. Revealing yourself.

I remember a few years ago when I was living in Florida and I thought I had before me a real friend, but all it took was one wicked crying session (I had a broken heart at the time) and she was gone. She wasn't up to the task of being reminded of her own vast wealth of emotional ocean. Other, better, friends came into my life, but I'll never forget the realization that who I thought she was never existed.

Moon Pluto Magic for liberating is sweat and tears and more tears and having a witness to your pain. Remember, the spiritual isn't separate from your normal, regular daily life. It isn't separate from you. They are the same.

Moon Pluto Magic for Transforming

None of these Moon Pluto Magics is better than any other. It depends on who you are and what you need. Many of us need them all. I think as you read through this section, you'll know what fits you. Your body will tell you.

You may read this chapter and think: *Hell yes, I need to truly transform my feelings, turn my intense emotions into something else, something bigger than me, something outside of me.*

Indeed, this is a far bigger job than soothing or letting go (even though those strategies matter and we need them). It's a bigger job because it's a life path itself. If you see yourself in this chapter, you know that the urge to transform your emotional bones and blood can't be avoided. And you likely already know if this is you. Moon Pluto Magic for you isn't mere strategies for emotional rebalance or spiritual clarity or calm for the hard times, but your very survival is at stake. It's a matter of life and death.

This is the path of the Witch, the artist, and the healer, and it's why this magic exists.

Transforming, Creating, Blasting

We all have times of transient grief or heartbreak or tough transitions, such as moving or a job change. Someone dies. We get sick. We lose something we wanted to keep. Often, the consoling or liberating kind of Moon Pluto Magic can help you with the painful reality of normal life. However, the obsessive need to take those feelings and turn them into gold? This requires more.

This magic is like the fiery Wands suit of the tarot. You aren't just pouring out like the watery Cups, no matter how forceful the pour, and you aren't discovering stillness like the earthy and rooted Pentacles suit, which seeds and plants. Instead, you are fire, breaking free.

Have you ever seen a house burn down? When I lived in Florida, one of my neighbors watched his beloved home turn to ash. The smoke rose, blackening the sky. Fire doesn't only destroy though. It lights our way.

Transforming Moon Pluto Magic may help you with:

• The persistent feeling that you are a Witch.

• Understanding you *need* to make art.

• The need for a spiritual path that isn't afraid of you.

Transforming Moon Pluto Magic isn't for occasional moods or situations that are assuaged by simple (or not so simple) solutions, but is chosen as a life path, spiritual road, because it's *who you are*. You are committed to the fearless one inside you, intrepid emotional explorer, creator.

••• ℌOMEWORK •••

THREE TO TRANSFORM

Are you a Witch? An artist? A healer? All three?

The Witch

That you can't *not* be a Witch. And you'll hear me say throughout this section: if you have discovered that you are a Witch (or artist or healer), *you have no choice.* None. You are bound.

Yes, there are some Witches who don't do magic, don't cast spells, don't talk to spirits, don't summon the dead, and yes, there are Witches for whom witching is seasonal, occasional, and not a way of life, day in, day out. But not you. You *must* do it.

You've spent a lifetime feeling what you feel, *dying* from what you feel, wrestling with your wild emotions, until that brilliant fated moment when you stumbled upon a book or a phrase or a teacher and *you knew.* You suddenly, finally knew who and what you were and you started on a path.

If you were smart, you learned how to caress those feelings and harness those feelings, and it made you powerful. Magic is an art, but for you so much more. It's the blood in your veins.

And it's those big, big emotions, now mastered, that make your spell craft so ferocious.

The Artist

Maybe you build furniture. Maybe you write dirty novels. Maybe you create painful, violent dances that express your turbulent emotional landscape. Maybe you scream into the void with your stand-up comedy. You *have* to make art. You *have* to make people hear you. You have to take your feelings *out* of your body and give them

a home, a form, a structure, outside of you: canvas, page, song.

You suffer when you don't do it, and it's a long road. Life-long. You don't stop. You keep creating. No choice. Or you'll die. That's how it feels.

With this type of Moon Pluto Magic, as Witch or artist, you are taking your emotions and putting them through a grinder. They have to be transformed. It's the burning-house story from above. You must be changed by fire and come out the other side, into light.

Whatever you create, it wasn't there before and now it is. The house burned down and then the man rebuilt. He gave birth to a new home. As an artist, you give birth to a work of art. As a Witch, you give birth to new reality. It's your very emotional intensity that makes your art so relentless.

The Healer

The transformation that I am talking about in this chapter, you don't just do it for yourself, but for others, because you are here to help others with your magic and your art. The work of healing calls to you, whether you like it or not, whether you want it or not. You may not think of yourself as a helper or in service to people at all, but it's the crucial step in this branch of Moon Pluto Magic, that you share and teach what you intrinsically understand.

You can't just make art and hide it in your room. You must share it with the world. They need you. And you can't just do your own spells all alone in the attic but must show others how. They also need you. You are the fire. You are the light of wisdom from the burning house, and I know this may make you uncomfortable. Why would anyone want all those roiling, boiling feelings and failures and stories of crippling emotional intensity? And yet they do. Helping others heals you. It heals you both.

BIG SPELLS FOR BIG FEELINGS.

MAGIC SPELLS FOR TUMULTUOUS SOULS

It's snowing in the big city as I write to you. It was supposed to be a light snow, but from my living room window I see it has covered the tops of the houses. It's as though each roof got a new coat of pristine, white paint while we were sleeping. Any weather can be good weather for a spell.

Spells, however, don't always mean sitting in your house with a candle and a few choice words, no matter how snowy the morning. You can take them into the world. The spells in this section seek to engage your body as well as your thinking, your busy mind.

If you try these spells, do remember that you are indeed doing magic, that there is a sacred, spiritual, special intention here and that what may appear on the surface to be ordinary activity is anything but.

One more thing: if these spells seem like meditations to you, it's because they are. Moon Pluto Magic doesn't draw a bold line between different spiritual techniques but knows they flow together. Sometimes a spell is a meditation, and a meditation is a spell. It all runs in the same direction. Many roads, one road.

Read the spells all the way through before beginning.

••• 𝕳OMEWORK •••

MAKE ME A RIVER (MOON PLUTO MAGIC FOR CONSOLING)

You'll need:

Ingredient List

A body of water

An empty jar or bottle

Your imagination

Time (depending on how far away the body of water)

I love this spell for when I've lost my inner peace and need to find it. This spell will put it back where it belongs.

Find a body of water. It doesn't matter if it's an ocean or a brook or your bathtub (running water is preferred though). Make sure you have at least fifteen minutes. Bring a small bottle or jar with you.

Look at the water. See yourself reflected in it. Imagine that the water is love. *Know* that the water is love. Imagine this water running all around you, surrounding you, filling you. It moves through your bones and cells. It hugs your blood. You are being filled with love. Your heart is being filled with love.

After fifteen minutes (longer if you wish), fill your jar with this love water. Once you're back home, put the bottle on your altar or in another special place. Gaze at the water in the bottle. See yourself reflected in it. You can do this anytime.

When you do any spells or mediations or other spiritual work in the near future, remember this day by the water, and how you felt filled with love and the water ran all around you.

Repeat three times: *I am love.* Note how it makes you feel to say this. If you have trouble getting the words out, note that. If you hesitate because you think it's silly, note that. Note if you say the words and don't believe them.

Try substituting the words *I love you.* Say it three times. Note if this feels better or easier.

Repeat this spell at least twice a month, or additional times when you need calming or soothing.

FIRE, BURN WHAT I CANNOT KEEP (MOON PLUTO MAGIC FOR LIBERATING)

You'll need:

Ingredient List

Paper and pen
The time/energy to take an emotional inventory
Matches or lighter

Fireproof plate or bowl

Small paper bag

A faraway place, ideally with a mountain peak and wind

I love this spell for when I have a feeling that's hung around too long, and I want to shift my energy from stagnant or sad into not necessarily happy ASAP, but at least better, even empowered. You will feel a palpable shift if you do this.

Please note this spell uses fire. Please practice fire safety.

Take an inventory of your life: how you've been feeling and how those feelings have been impacting you. Think about any feelings or states of mind or situations that you cannot keep and should leave your life. Make sure you include only what *must* go.

On a piece of paper, the size of an index card or smaller, write down the feelings or states of mind or situations that you want to wholeheartedly dump or destroy, without ambivalence or ambiguity or sentimentality. Did anything change when you went from only thinking about it to writing it down? Take your time. Include anything you want to dump: poverty, lack of faith, jealousy, bad job, obnoxious neighbors, low self-esteem, rotten relationship, fake friends, failure.

Burn the paper (or pages, if you couldn't stop writing). Collect the ashes in a small paper bag.

Get thyself to a faraway place. Go as far as you can go. When no one is looking, cast out your ashes to the wind (best on a mountain peak). If this is impractical for you, you can always toss the bag of ashes in a garbage can, just make sure it's far from where you live, far enough so that it felt like you entered a new land to dispose of it.

After the ashes are gone, say this word three times: *goodbye.*

··· 𝔥OMEWORK ···

I AM AN ARTIST (MOON PLUTO MAGIC FOR TRANSFORMING)

You'll need:

Ingredient List

Your favorite music and headphones or earbuds

No demands on your time for at least forty minutes

Privacy (or one room where you won't be disturbed)

Extra-large sketch pad and crayons or markers or pastels or charcoal

Timer

I love this spell for when I *need* to create (to let my intense emotions out), but also need a break from any serious artistic projects or other work I have going on. You don't need to leave the house for this one. There are no complex instructions. You just need paper, something to draw with, a little music, and a little privacy. You can go longer than forty minutes if you want. Getting lost in the moment is recommended.

Choose your favorite songs that make you feel your feelings: happy, sad, elated, memory lane, raging, lustful, and/or any others. It's fine if the emotions overlap. You want songs that will kick up the emotional dust in you. It's okay for that dust to get in your eyes. It's okay if you cry. It's okay if you skip songs. Get your songs ready.

Then, start to draw. Do this for fifteen minutes. Set a timer. No rules, no instructions, no boundaries. Just see where the paper and mood take you. It may turn into a story, like a comic. You may just scribble. A self-portrait may take over. You might draw tarot cards that don't yet exist.

After fifteen minutes is up, start a new page, but this time you are drawing the feeling that is most dominant. Again, no extra rules or instructions for what to draw or how to draw, just that you are drawing that feeling and letting the music guide you. Do this with passion.

After those fifteen minutes are up, close your sketch pad. Put away your writing tools. No need to review what you've done. You can turn off the music or leave it on. Tidy your workspace. Make it look as if you were never there. You can even sweep it with your broom (real or imaginary) if you have time.

Then, slowly, walk around the room you were drawing in, or walk around your entire home or apartment (as long as you have privacy and no one will interrupt you). Walk around your space knowing that with each step you are sealing, finalizing this transformation process, that you've taken the unruly, intense emotions and turned them into lines and colors on a page. Those feelings have left your body.

Then, tap the walls of the room lightly with your fingertips. Do this a few times. Tap the windows and windowsills. Touch the floor. Reach up high, on your toes if you are able, as though you could touch the ceiling. Stretch both arms out, tilt your head back, and look up.

Say this three times, out loud: *I am home. I am here.*

The spell is complete.

AND NOW WE NEED
THE TAROT ONCE MORE.

TAROT MAGIC
FOR EMOTIONAL INTENSITY

Let's return now to where we started, the Magic Cafe, my home away from home. The coffee is better than usual this morning and tastes like they shipped it in from a golden land. It may be too good for us tired city people, too sleepy to tell the difference between muddy water and best in show. I order another. It's fuel for the day, and it's still winter in the city, cold and dry and sunless. The sky this morning may be bleak, but we have our beloved tarot to keep us warm, and this morning it's tarot for Moon Pluto Magic, which is tarot magic for our emotions.

The following card spreads will help us investigate the private places of our feelings, their secrets, pry them open. What is it that your feelings *du jour* require? These tarot spreads will help you figure it out.

INSTRUCTIONS FOR WINTER
MAGIC–CAFE TAROT

You can put these tarot spreads in any shape you wish: a horseshoe, a heart, a straight line, a diagonal, little rows. Whatever moves you.

Experiment. Lately, I've been using oval shapes when I do a multicard spread.

You can do these anytime, day or night. You can do them in public, like I do, or in private, alone, or with a friend. You can share them with your coven, if you have one. You can start a coven with these tarot spreads in mind. You can do them by the light of the moon or in the pitch-dark, switching the light on your smartphone on and off. I have been this person, yes.

When you do these tarot spreads and start to translate the meanings of the cards for yourself, you can read the cards literally, using a guidebook, and stop there.

You can use your intuition and not pay attention to codified meanings. You can combine these two approaches.

You can even pull apart these tarot spreads and answer just one or two of the questions instead of all of them. Of course, I suggest you take notes as you go so that you can read over your findings later. I just bought two thick journals for this very purpose.

And you can try to do these tarot spreads in a cursory way, but I think if you go slow, they will take you as deep and wide as intended, as the questions prefer.

••• 𝕳OMEWORK •••

TAROT MAGIC FOR EMOTIONAL INTENSITY

These tarot spreads are for the emotions of the moment. Do them when you feel sad or heavy or dark or anxious. Do them when you feel not quite right and aren't sure what to do. You don't need to wait until the house is burning down. You can start when you feel a little warm or the match is struck. The cards are always here for you. The cards are always wise. They may confuse sometimes, but if you take your time, the answers arise. You may even wind up creating your own Moon Pluto Magic spreads. I hope you do.

The Discovery: What Do I Need Right Now (Eight Cards)

What is best for me at this time: consoling, liberating, or transforming my emotions?

Give me a little more detail.

What action should I take?

How else can I best care for myself at this time?

What do my emotions need from me?

Is Moon Pluto Magic what I need today?

Is there other advice you have, dear beloved tarot?

Finally, is there anything else I should I be doing?

The Peace: Tarot Spread for Calming Emotions (Four Cards)

Show me one thing I need to do right now to feel calm.

Show me one thing I need to think right now to feel calm.

Show me one thing I need to know *right now to feel calm.*

Show me one thing I need to trust *right now to feel calm.*

The Root: Tarot Spread for Releasing Emotions (Five Cards)

What is the root of my unrest at this time?

What does the root need from me?

Do I need to release these intense emotions?

How can I best release my intense emotions?

Is there another strategy that will also help me?

The Art: Tarot Spread for Transforming Emotions (Six Cards)

Is creativity (including magic) the right strategy for me at this time?

If yes, then what kind of creativity? Show me.

If no, then what will help?

Show me the art (or magic) I need to create.

Show me the artist I am now.

Show me the artist I am to become.

Plan for Emotional Peace (Seven Cards)

Show me a good plan for bringing emotional peace to my life.

Do I need a teacher or mentor?

Show me details about this teacher or mentor. (Or alternately, show me the strategy if no teacher is required.)

Short-term outcome of this plan.

Long-term outcome of this plan (pull extra card if outcome is ambiguous or troubling).

What else is needed?

Wild card: show me what I haven't thought of yet.

WE'VE REACHED THE LAST STOP ON OUR JOURNEY, DEAR SEEKERS. IT'S HARD TO SAY GOODBYE. I HAVE A FEW MORE WORDS FOR YOU. REMEMBER THAT ANCIENT ASTROLOGER WE MET EARLIER? SHE'S BACK. BUT FIRST, A RECOMMENDATION FROM MY MOON PLUTO MAGIC SUITCASE.

Recommendations:
In my Moon Pluto Magic Suitcase

My suitcase here isn't the same as the others. It's empty. For the moment. I'd love for you to fill it yourself—because what comforts us (which is what Moon Pluto Magic is all about) is so individual that I can't give you more specifics than what I already did in these chapters themselves. What soothes us or sets us free, emotionally, is far more personal than a recommended tarot book where you're mostly getting information, no matter how poetic or insightful.

I can send you in the right direction, though, which is this: your physical body and your emotional body are the recommendations here, the resources you need most. You're never without them. Your *self* itself, and all its brazen, maddening wants and needs and deep, deep desires and feelings, is the great "book" I recommend, the best book of all, which will tell you, without fail, everything you need to know.

Conclusion

During the writing of this book, I started dreaming about that ancient astrologer. Remember her? We first met her in the astrology chapters. I'll leave it up to you to go find her.

These dreams, at first, came every once in a while and then every night, all night. They were detailed, vivid dreams, unlike any I'd ever experienced. I took it as a sign. I was meant to share more of her story.

This One Recurring Dream

In the dream, I'm in a room. Whose room I do not know. And on a large, oak table, in this room, I find a little black book, and it's her book (somehow I know this in the dream), and it's her handwriting, and it's a diary, and as I'm turning the pages, the pages disappear in my hands. Turn a page, *poof*. Turn a page, *poof*. The book is alive, so it seems, moving, disappearing, returning, pulsating. It's as though the book has wings. I swear I can hear them rustling.

And let me tell you something else, more strange than any dream image. Sometimes, in waking life, over these

months, I'd wonder whether these really were *dreams*. If not, what
were they?

But there I am in the dream, reading her book, and she's writing about *that night*. The night she ran from her magical labora-
tory, abandoning all her books and papers and potions and charts.
The images come fast. I see her traveling on foot, then stagecoach,
then horseback. I see her crossing miles of river and road. Time
and place start skipping faster, and there she is, at a tavern, talking
magic. There she is, spending the night at a hotel, doing astrology
for curious strangers. There she is, laying down cards in the middle of nowhere, a dark wood. Then, more places and more roads,
and she just keeps going. I would wake up exhausted each time, my
head filled with her life and travels.

And then. Then came the night that I realized I hadn't been
dreaming at all, but instead, well, I don't know what to call it. I'll
just tell you, plainly, what happened. I woke up one bright Sunday
morning to see the very book I'm telling you about here, the book
I had been dreaming of, night after night. It was there on my night
table. And I heard the sound of wings.

ᴀ ᴘʀᴏᴍɪsᴇ

The first time I had this dream I thought, *This is us*. We are all on this weird life voyage, journey, road, adventure, quest, seeking answers, just like her, over miles of river, miles of road, searching for meaning and truth! Books are good guides, but eventually we just need to go, to *move*!

Have you decided, dear reader? Do any of these practices, rituals, routines, spells, experiments, pit stops belong on your spiritual path? It's the question we've been asking since page one, day one. Tarot, astrology, spirit, magic, and Moon Pluto plans for your emotional soul. Have you started dreaming about them? You will. I think you will.

And, if nothing else, I hope these words get you thinking about what *is* for you, what belongs to you, spiritually, magically, mystically. Fill that collection of cool stuff up, up, up to the top. And you, too, may dream a magical book into existence.

··· ʜᴏᴍᴇᴡᴏʀᴋ ···

HERE'S ONE LAST TAROT SPREAD FOR THE ROAD

Do this one after you've read the entire book. It's a four-card spread.

What's the most important spiritual practice I should take on the road with me?

What's the second most important spiritual practice I should take on the road with me?

How do I start these adventures?

Where will these adventures take me?

NOW YOU'RE ON YOUR OWN,
DEAR STAR LOVERS. YOUR COMPANY
HAS MEANT THE WORLD TO ME.
GOODBYE, FOR NOW, AND GOOD LUCK.

ℙOSTCARD FROM THE ℰPICENTER

I wrote this book before coronavirus. I wrote it before the phrase *social distancing* entered our lives. And I finished the first round of edits right before the pandemic took hold of America.

Our lives are changing, possibly, forever.

What will life look like a year from now? What will be the fate of the city I love? And another, more personal, question: Will either of us live to see the publication of this book? As I type to you, that's the vibe around here. We don't know what will happen, and, as of this writing, New York is the epicenter of the crisis.

This isn't drama, but reality. There is no vaccine (yet), and treatments are experimental. We haven't yet flattened the curve (another phrase popularized in early 2020).

One irony that struck me as I finished those first edits was that much of this book is like a love letter—not only to magic and spiritual seeking, but to New York City, its streets now empty except for workers considered essential, including our grocery clerks and nurses, and those of us going outside for long walks and fresh air.

And as I was writing the book, sentence by sentence, chapter by chapter, I was planning it all out: where to take you each day, which street, which subway, which moment of daily life and magic to share with you. And to locate us there, in that world. Will we stop sitting in cafes, reading and writing and tarot-ing? I pray not. I pray as you read this that you are sitting in a beautiful place you love, at home or out in the world. That you survived. That I did too.

Here in my Brooklyn quarantine, I still go out for solitary walks. I get takeout instead of eating in. I do all my tarot spreads at home. But I hope by the time you read this, we're together again at the Magic Cafe, marveling at how much the world has changed and how much has remained the same.

One thing I know for sure: as long as there are humans wandering the earth, there will be stories and there will be magic and there will be community and there will be love. I will meet you there.

April / Nisan 2020

To Write to the Author

If you wish to contact the author or would like more information about this book, please write to the author in care of Llewellyn Worldwide Ltd. and we will forward your request. Both the author and publisher appreciate hearing from you and learning of your enjoyment of this book and how it has helped you. Llewellyn Worldwide Ltd. cannot guarantee that every letter written to the author can be answered, but all will be forwarded. Please write to:

Aliza Einhorn
℅ Llewellyn Worldwide
2143 Wooddale Drive
Woodbury, MN 55125-2989
Please enclose a self-addressed stamped envelope for reply,
or $1.00 to cover costs. If outside the USA, enclose
an international postal reply coupon.

Many of Llewellyn's authors have websites with additional information and resources. For more information, please visit our website at http://www.llewellyn.com.